Disabled Women and Domestic Violence

Disabled Women and Domestic Violence

Responding to the Experiences of Survivors

Ravi K. Thiara, Gill Hague, Ruth Bashall,
Brenda Ellis and Audrey Mullender

Foreword by Nicola Harwin CBE

Jessica Kingsley *Publishers*
London and Philadelphia

First published in 2012
by Jessica Kingsley Publishers
116 Pentonville Road
London N1 9JB, UK
and
400 Market Street, Suite 400
Philadelphia, PA 19106, USA

www.jkp.com

Library of Congress Cataloging in Publication Data
A CIP catalog record for this book is available from the Library of Congress

British Library Cataloguing in Publication Data
A CIP catalogue record for this book is available from the British Library

ISBN 978 1 84905 008 1
eISBN 978 0 85700 558 8

Printed and bound in Great Britain

To all disabled women who are survivors of domestic violence, for their courage and determination, and to disabled women across the world who are working together against violence.

To Simon for all his love and support.
(Audrey Mullender)

To Vijayatara (Dr Sharon Smith) who taught me that violence does not have to control our lives and wise women can laugh.
(Ruth Bashall)

Contents

Foreword   9
Nicola Harwin CBE

ACKNOWLEDGEMENTS   11

Chapter 1   Introduction   13

Chapter 2   What the Research Tells Us: A Story of Gaps
and Failings   25

Chapter 3   Disabled Women's Experiences of Domestic
Violence and Abuse   34

Chapter 4   Professional Responses to Disabled Women
Affected by Domestic Violence   56

Chapter 5   Understanding Our History: The Personal is Political   82
Brenda Ellis and Ruth Bashall

Chapter 6   Nothing About Us Without Us: Policy and Practice   106
Ruth Bashall and Brenda Ellis

Chapter 7   Ideas for Moving Forward: Good Practice and
Recommendations   137

Chapter 8   Strategic Agendas: Incorporating Issues for Disabled
              Women Experiencing Domestic Violence   155

Chapter 9   Conclusions   169

              APPENDIX: STUDY METHODOLOGY   174

              ABOUT THE AUTHORS   178

              REFERENCES   180

              SUBJECT INDEX   187

              AUTHOR INDEX   192

Foreword

Since the early 1970s, feminist activists and survivors of sexual and domestic violence, working together, have helped pioneer significant changes in the way that violence against women and children is understood and responded to within public policy, and we have seen the development of a network of specialist services across the UK.

From the beginning, a commitment to equality and human rights has been the cornerstone of our analysis of gender abuse and of the requirements for service delivery. Yet, despite our best intentions and undoubted improvements in accessibility of services, the voices and needs of disabled women experiencing domestic or sexual abuse have received little real attention in strategic developments on violence against women at either local or national level. Equally, the need to address gender-based violence has not been a priority for most mainstream disability organisations, despite the strenuous efforts of some committed disabled women activists.

This book is itself an example of that uphill struggle: it took nearly a decade to achieve the funding to undertake the research upon which this book is based, despite numerous attempts by disabled women researchers. This book also, therefore, represents a triumph of their commitment and perseverance.

Women's Aid was proud to have had the opportunity to partner with members of the research team and the Advisory Group, supported by funding from the Big Lottery. The findings of the research and the contents of this book set out clearly the tasks and priorities ahead. Disabled women face multiple challenges and discrimination, both in their experiences of domestic and sexual violence, and in gaining access to appropriate services. The common experiences of all victims of domestic and sexual abuse (such as not being believed or being unable to get effective help and support) are compounded by unhelpful stereotypes about disabled women, and their impairments are used by abusers to increase the abuser's power and disabled women's vulnerability and isolation.

I hope this book will be a wake-up call for professionals and activists in all relevant statutory and voluntary agencies to review our own policy approaches and ensure that in all our local consultations and strategic planning, the findings and messages in this book, and the voices of disabled women survivors, are heard.

Nicola Harwin CBE
Chief Executive
Women's Aid

Acknowledgements

We are very grateful to Women's Aid for initiating and managing the research on which this book is based, and to the Big Lottery who funded the study. Especial thanks to current and former Women's Aid staff, Nicola Harwin, Nikki Norman, Jackie Barron and Emma Williamson, for all their input.

Our sincerest thanks to the Advisory Group and disabled women consultants who advised the research, for their time, advice and guidance, especially Anne Pridmore, then Chair of the UK Disabled People Council, Jenny Morris and Jane Bethall. We are also particularly grateful for the help of many agencies, professionals and activists in the disability and the domestic violence fields for taking the time to speak to us, respond to surveys, and for giving us valuable contacts. A special thank you for their particular contributions to Jacky Gruhn, Cassie Hague, Dave Merrick and Mel Turner.

Most of all, our heartfelt thanks to all the disabled women domestic violence survivors who participated in the national research as advisers, in focus groups, in workshops and in interviews. Their generosity in being part of this project and their moving experiences are key to this book. We hope that their advice and recommendations for improvements in services for abused disabled women will be realised.

Chapter 1

Introduction

Domestic violence in intimate relationships blights societies, and the lives of individuals, across the world. It pervades all known communities. Look up and down the road or street where you live, for example. You may not realise it is there, but it is. Where domestic abuse is happening, it is likely to be behind the doors and windows, in bedrooms and sitting rooms and kitchens, but it is also there on the street or in places where couples, and adult men and women, meet socially (see Hague and Malos 2005). On the positive side, since the early 1980s, support services for women and children facing domestic violence (and more limited projects for men) have begun to be established in many countries. There are not nearly enough of them, but at least they exist. In the UK, there are refuges, outreach services, government policies, criminal justice responses, children's services, counselling projects, at least some housing options for victims, and partnership strategies across localities which the relevant agencies are tasked to work within. But not, it seems, if you are disabled.

Services specifically for disabled women experiencing intimate abuse are thin on the ground in the UK, according to small-scale research conducted in the 1990s and 2000s (see, for example, James-Hanman 1994; Trotter, Radford and Harne 2007). This book is about disabled women's experiences of domestic violence and abuse, about the lack of services and about the small amount of good practice which does already exist and could be built on for the future. It is the first book on this subject in the UK and it has been a long time coming.

In fact, it has taken almost 30 years, from the early 1980s, for disabled women to begin to be taken seriously by the domestic violence movement, while awareness of intimate personal abuse within disabled people's organisations has only recently begun. However, this book is part of a new attention to the issue and our aim is that it will contribute to the development of new services and a new awareness. We need as a society to start to take on the needs of disabled women in terms of domestic abuse in a dedicated

– rather than a peripheral – way. The hope is that the book may act as a catalyst in this process.

What the book is about

Throughout this book, we will use and be informed by the first-ever national study in the UK on the needs of disabled women experiencing domestic violence and abuse, and the services available to meet those needs. Conducted between 2005 and 2009, this was a pioneering study which attempted to break new ground. We draw on its findings extensively. The book also contains chapters by two prominent disabled activists and practitioners on the issues faced by abused disabled women.

Linking our discussions mainly to the national study, we will detail previous research on the issue, the impacts of domestic abuse on disabled women, the services currently available, the gaps in those services, and disabled women's advice to other women and to helping agencies. Further, we will look at examples of good practice, government strategies, the policy and service developments that we need to improve responses to abused disabled women, and practical recommendations for change. Where we can, we draw directly on the words of disabled women who have experienced domestic violence and abuse. The book is written for a wider, rather than an academic, audience but is rooted in research and practice evidence throughout.

Terminology

Before we start to develop the arguments and discussions of the book, it is important to define the words we are using. Most importantly, this means asking how we understand 1) disability, and 2) domestic violence.

It is important to be aware that the use of the term 'people with disabilities' is regarded as poor practice in the UK in the disabled people's movement, and increasingly across the board. It is also significant to note, though, that in the United States, Canada, Australia and many other countries, the opposite is the case, and the term is the favoured one and widely used. However, in the UK 'disabled' is the word of choice – as used, for example, in the term 'disabled women', rather than 'women with disabilities'. Learning from the disabled people's movement and from disabled activists in this country, it has become good practice here always to use the term 'disability' in the singular as describing the impacts of a discriminating society, rather than as a word to refer to the individual conditions or impairments that people may have. In this book, we have therefore used these terms throughout.

Disability as a political issue: the social model versus the medical model

Ways in which disability is defined and explained remain highly contested between the medical and social explanatory models. In the medical model, disabled people are viewed through the prism of their impairments or medical conditions and the assumed dependency that results. Also known as the 'individual model', the medical model may result in the exclusion of disabled people from society, through an emphasis on the need for the individual disabled person to adapt to society, where control is often vested in professionals rather than disabled people themselves (Brisenden 1986; Oliver 1996; Shakespeare 1998). By contrast, the social model within which this book is grounded argues that the problems experienced by disabled people, and disability itself, result from socially disabling attitudes and practices which aggravate the impact of the person's physical condition (Shakespeare and Watson 1997; UPIAS 1976).

The social model acknowledges the existence of impairments that disabled people live with and tries to avoid simplistic explanations. Nonetheless, without minimising the importance of individual conditions, proponents of this model argue that it is society that lets disabled people down. A clear distinction is drawn between impairment and disability.

Back in 1976, the Union of the Physically Impaired Against Segregation (UPIAS) in the UK developed a pioneering definition of disability as:

> The disadvantage or restriction of activity caused by contemporary social organisation which takes little or no account of people who have physical impairments and thus excludes them from participation in the mainstream of social activities. (UPIAS 1976)

In this book, we have broadly adopted this activist definition and position, and it is also further discussed in Chapter 5. However, the social model is now fairly widely accepted. Even major definitions of disability used globally now acknowledge it on some level. For example, the World Health Organisation's International Classification of Functioning, Disability and Health, the international measure of disability, which is endorsed by all 191 WHO member states, takes into account social factors and does not view disability only as a medical or biological dysfunction (WHO 2009).

Thus, the theoretical basis of the study is grounded in an understanding that it is barriers caused by social attitudes to disability, and by a lack of commitment to the issue, which have contributed to society's failure to take account of the needs of disabled people. It is this failure that is truly disabling, and not people's individual conditions (Corker and Thomas

2002; Shakespeare and Watson 1997; Swain *et al.* 2004). The book also adheres to the important, and on occasion inspiring, principle of the disabled people's equality movement: 'Nothing about us without us' (Charlton 1998). All practice and policy developments, and awareness-raising and training, can only be achieved with leadership from disabled people, often but not necessarily in partnership with the non-disabled. In our research, we attempted to develop further understandings of the social model in relation to abused women's experiences and the exclusions that they face – which are often multiplied if they are disabled.

What is domestic violence/domestic abuse?

In this book, we will use the terms domestic violence and domestic abuse more or less interchangeably. The national study which informs the book throughout was managed by Women's Aid, the national domestic violence charity, as further discussed later, and we use the Women's Aid definition of domestic abuse as:

> physical, psychological, sexual or financial violence that takes place within an intimate or family-type relationship and forms a pattern of coercive and controlling behaviour. This can include forced marriage and so-called 'honour' crimes. Domestic violence often includes a range of abusive behaviours, not all of which are in themselves inherently 'violent'. (Women's Aid 2007)

Thus, so-called 'honour'-based violence and forced marriage (as opposed to arranged marriage in which the parties consent) are currently regarded as issues of domestic violence (see Gangoli, Razak and McCarry 2006; Gill 2006), and many definitions now contain a reference to coercive control, sometimes continual and long-term, by the abuser over the abused (see Stark 2007).

There is some agreement among organisations addressing gendered violence across the world, including Women's Aid in the UK, that women may experience intimate violence regardless of ethnicity, religion, class, caste, age, sexuality, disability or lifestyle, although it may take a variety of cultural forms. Domestic violence can occur in a range of relationships including those which are heterosexual, gay, lesbian, bisexual or transgendered, and also within extended families (Women's Aid 2007). Most researchers and policy-makers, as well as specialist agencies, agree that the vast majority of intimate violence is experienced by women. Perpetrators are most commonly men, although abuse can also occur the other way round (see, for example, Gadd *et al.* 2002; Hester 2009). Thus, while individuals requesting assistance from helping agencies will overwhelmingly be women, this is not to belittle the need of male victims for appropriate help and support. In this book, however, we discuss domestic violence against women specifically. This type of intimate violence includes sexual assault and rape within intimate relationships as well as physical, financial and emotional abuse, and is distressingly widespread. The various definitions may mention domestic violence and disability in passing, but none are wide enough to incorporate disabled women's experiences of abuse in any adequate way.

Most studies in a variety of countries find that around one in four women experience physical domestic violence across a lifetime, with one in eight to one in ten experiencing intimate abuse of this type at any one time (Hague and Malos 2005; Women's Aid 2007). A pioneering international study of domestic violence across many countries, the *Multi-country Study of Health and Domestic Violence Against Women*, was conducted by the World Health Organisation and completed in 2005 (WHO 2005). The study was based on interviews with 24,000 women by carefully trained interviewers over 15 sites and 10 countries, namely: Bangladesh, Brazil, Ethiopia, Japan, Peru, Namibia, Samoa, Serbia and Montenegro, Thailand and the United Republic of Tanzania. The research was also replicated by New Zealand, with closely related surveys in Chile, China, Indonesia and Vietnam, and concluded that violence against women is extremely widespread and demands a public health response across the world. This study showed very high levels of physical domestic violence globally, being experienced by between 29 per cent and 62 per cent of women, with the comparable figures for sexual violence being between 30 per cent and 56 per cent. Overall, the World Health Organisation informs us (WHO 2005) that between one in five and one in three women worldwide experience physical violence from their intimate partners – from the persons with whom they share perhaps their closest, most tender moments and who may profess to love them. It is worth reiterating this extremely high percentage – up to one in three of the world's women experience some form of intimate violence, as estimated by the most prestigious health organisation in the world.

We do not know how many women experiencing domestic violence are disabled in the UK, as there are almost no statistics available. What we do know is that very few abused disabled women are in a position to call the police for help, and only tiny numbers currently make use of domestic violence refuge and other services. However, in 2010, the Metropolitan Police in London estimated that approximately 3 per cent of their domestic violence referrals were from disabled women, and Women's Aid has estimated that about 7 per cent of the women they assist are disabled, as discussed in Chapter 4. However, both figures are known to be such an under-estimate as to be almost useless.

Looking at it from both sides: disability and domestic abuse

In taking an initial look at what this book is about, our aim is to build some integration between domestic violence and disability services. From a cursory look at the existing literature (which will be discussed in more detail in Chapter 2), it is fairly clear that domestic violence organisations and disability services tend to occupy two different worlds. Practitioners and agencies in these two arenas of social and welfare responses scarcely interact, either in this country or in others (see, for instance, Chenoweth 1997; Nixon 2009; Trotter *et al.* 2007). The domestic violence world tries to provide services for disabled women but appears to have few available. The disability equality world does not always consider people's gender as an important factor or take note of the prevalence of domestic violence. This book is predicated on the premise that it is vital to bring these two movements together. We aim in the book to reach out to both disability and domestic violence practitioners, policy-makers and activists, to urge them to come together in an informed way, if the experiences of abused disabled women are to be addressed. For too long, these issues have been 'siloed' in their own services and within separate social welfare arenas, with the result that disabled women experiencing violence have often slipped between the two sets of services.

This book, and the study on which it is based, takes the view that the disabled people's equality movement and its services, together with wider disability organisations, need to start to address domestic violence. Conversely, we view it as similarly important that the domestic violence movement – with its refuge, outreach and advocacy services, alongside the specialist criminal justice domestic violence responses that now exist – needs to build on what it has already done to further address the needs of disabled women and children systematically. It is only when this happens that things can improve. Further, we surmise that it is when the two sectors start to work constructively together and to learn from each other, alongside effective statutory health and social services, that real change for disabled women facing intimate abuse can truly begin. Our national study was designed to look at whether this analysis was right – and how everyone's practice could be taken forward.

The study on which the book is based

In more detail, then, the research which forms the backbone of this book arose because it became clear, throughout the 1990s and early 2000s, that there were only limited local studies in the UK on domestic violence and disabled women, and very few services (see, for example, James-Hanman

1994; Radford, Harne and Trotter 2006). Some disabled women activists had campaigned long and hard for the domestic violence movement and for available services for abuse survivors to take up the needs of disabled women, but their experience was that there seemed to be little interest (Ellis 1995). In the 2000s, Women's Aid, which represents domestic violence organisations and maintains a strong national presence working with government, as well as with activists and services, also became involved. As the principal organisation providing a wide range of local, refuge-based, outreach and support services to abused women and their children throughout the country, Women's Aid had become more and more aware, over the years, of difficulties in meeting disabled women's needs. Earlier research and research overviews (for example, Mullender and Hague 2000) revealed a dearth of studies or literature on the experiences of disabled women survivors of domestic violence (sometimes as a result of neglect or tokenism on the part of the researchers concerned). Even studies that had made a deliberate effort to give a 'voice' to abused women (for example, Hague, Mullender and Aris 2003) had not been able to encompass disabled women in any significant numbers. Thus, there appeared to be gaps in both services and awareness, but little systematic research or national data about the experiences of abused disabled women in the UK which could be used to provide a strong evidence base and to support proposals for change.

Women's Aid therefore decided to initiate national research to fill this gap through a dedicated study. However, this was easier said than done. For several years, Women's Aid, together with disabled women activists and some disability organisations, tried without any success in either the academic or the policy fields to raise dedicated funding. They were finally able to secure funding in 2005, through the generous sponsorship of the UK Big Lottery Fund, to conduct this national study on the needs of abused disabled women, and on the effectiveness of services provided.

The Violence Against Women Research Group (now the Gender and Violence Research Centre) at the University of Bristol and the Centre for the Study of Safety and Well-being at the University of Warwick were commissioned to conduct the research. Both of these UK research groups have a long history of conducting research on all aspects of violence against women. They were selected by Women's Aid to be named in the research bid on the grounds of their previous experience as activist-based research groups at the forefront of national and international gender violence work in the UK and their strong reputations in the field, as well as their previous experience of collaborating effectively together. Both groups work within an activist and feminist frame, and attempt, whenever possible, to raise the voices and views of women survivors and their children.

The aims of the study

The aims of the national study were to develop further understandings of the needs of abused disabled women, to investigate the scope of – and gaps in – existing provision, and to identify examples of good practice/policy in both the domestic violence and the disability fields. Building on these findings, the study aimed to produce research evidence, good practice guidance and policy recommendations, including making inputs into local and national strategic agendas, to support service improvement.

The focus of the research was on the fit, or the lack of it, between the way abuse is experienced by disabled women and the forms of help they would like to see in place, on the one hand, and the actual responses of policy-makers, practitioners in statutory agencies and specialist support organisations, on the other. A key element in this endeavour was to explore the extent to which women's organisations, such as Women's Aid and other relevant support services, are geared up to meet the needs of disabled women and, conversely, the extent to which disabled people's organisations are aware of, and able to deal with, domestic violence. The study also led to recommendations for policy, practice and strategic development which aimed to better equip practitioners and activists from both the domestic violence and the disability fields to offer effective help in the future.

This book will build on the study to reflect on disabled women's experiences of domestic abuse, to look at services, including the failings and gaps, to draw out wider service and policy implications and to discuss recommendations for change. It is aimed towards building awareness of abused disabled women's experiences and needs and, particularly, towards changing and improving practice. Thus, it is not designed as a theoretical text and our intentions do not include developing new conceptualisations or theorising on disability and domestic violence. The book will be useful to activists, policy-makers and practitioners, as well as to researchers and students. Disabled women have been excluded from many of the recent developments in services for women experiencing violence and abuse (see Magowan 2003). Our hope is that this book will be part of making a difference.

The methods used in the study

The mainly qualitative study which informs this book adopted throughout a woman-centred and activist approach, grounded in the long-standing evidence of the commonly-occurring abuse of women by their male intimates (for example, Dobash and Dobash 1992; Hague and Malos 2005; Schechter 1982; WHO 2005). The methods we used are mentioned briefly in this introduction but are discussed in detail in the Appendix.

The study was conducted between 2005 and 2008. An advisory group of disabled women consultants/activists was established and worked with the researchers, and the research was carried out by an all-women team of disabled and non-disabled women. Ethical approval and oversight were provided by the Universities of Bristol and Warwick, and Women's Aid which managed the research was involved closely in all stages. Overall financial management was provided by the University of Bristol working with Women's Aid.

The study used a multi-method strategy carried out in three stages, each of which built on the previous one. The first stage consisted of wide-ranging consultations with disabled women and with key experts, together with a nationally-convened focus group of disabled women, most of whom had experiences of intimate abuse. This was followed by two comprehensive national surveys. One was of local disabled people's organisations, although large national umbrella bodies working on disability were not covered (but some provided addresses of their members). The second survey was of local domestic violence services, including both refuge and outreach services. The surveys looked at the aids and adaptations for disabled women using the relevant agency, staff training, services offered, staff attitudes to disabled women and the extent to which the agency made use of multi-agency approaches and other services.

The second stage of the research built on the first by using the initial findings to inform in-depth and lengthy individual interviews with 30 abused disabled women from diverse backgrounds in terms of ethnicity, sexuality, and socio-economic status. Careful attention was paid to each woman's needs, impairments and the extreme sensitivity of the issues. This sample was only achieved after repeated and very time-consuming efforts over many months, and one of the issues which came out of the study was the extreme difficulty of reaching disabled women experiencing abuse. We interviewed the women about the impact that disability had had on the violence they had experienced, the perpetrators of the abuse, the woman's ability to respond to abusive situations, the impact on any children involved, the nature of any help-seeking they had engaged in, the responses received, the advice which they would offer to other disabled abused women, and their views on good practice.

In the third stage, ideas for good practice were developed from the interviews, and examples of organisations using such practice were identified to conduct good practice case studies of these organisations. The case studies and the findings of the first two stages, together with a further set of interviews with commissioning officers working at the more strategic level, were then further built on to evolve good practice and policy recommendations. These recommendations covered improving services, and both policy and strategic development. They have been found to be helpful by practitioners and policy-makers and were summarised in both a major report and a good practice guide, available from Women's Aid (Hague *et al.* 2008a, 2008b; see also the list of reports at the end of the References). The book will summarise these recommendations for the benefit, we hope, of people working in the field.

Which women and which perpetrators are included?

In this book, we focus specifically on the experiences of women exposed to domestic abuse who have physical and sensory impairments, including older women. This is due to the limitations of the funding for the national study on which it is based. We strongly recognise that abuse is a major issue for women with learning difficulties and with mental health issues. Unfortunately, though, we did not have the resources to address or explore the experiences of women in these situations in either the study or the book. In fact, two further comprehensive studies would be required. However, we recognise the importance of these issues and believe that funding must be raised in the future to conduct further robust and comprehensive research on the needs of women in the UK with learning difficulties and mental health issues who are experiencing domestic violence and abuse.

The book contains wide-ranging material about disabled women and domestic violence, particularly in Chapters 5 and 6, which are general contributions and are not specifically based on the research. For the study itself, the team made a particular effort to include disabled lesbians experiencing abuse and disabled women from black, minority ethnic and refugee (BMER) communities, especially including South Asian and African-Caribbean women. Older women have been included where possible.

As far as the perpetrators of abuse are concerned, we include the needs of disabled women experiencing intimate abuse from partners, ex-partners, other family members, or paid personal assistants and carers. Thus, we understand that abuse from intimates includes experiences of violence and intimidation from paid carers and assistants, a particularly neglected subject, though we did not have the resources to investigate abuse perpetrated by workers in residential homes and institutions.

Overall, then, the aim of this book, and of the national study, is to fill a major gap in existing knowledge in the UK by further developing understandings of the needs of abused disabled women and the scope of existing provision in terms of strategic, policy and practice development. The study draws on a growing view that the voices and perspectives of those who use services, in this case disabled women who have experienced intimate abuse, should inform the evaluation of these services and the development of best practice guidance (for example, Dullea and Mullender 1999; Hague *et al.* 2003). In this book, we subscribe to this view, drawing on the voices of disabled women, and particularly disabled women who have used services to try to address domestic violence.

What the chapters of the book contain

Chapter 2 will discuss what we know about domestic violence and disabled women from the previous research on which our study built. The following chapters will discuss the study and our findings in detail. By drawing on the accounts of disabled women, Chapter 3 gives voice to the women in our study and outlines, in detail, their experiences of domestic violence and abuse perpetrated by intimate partners, family members and paid carers. The chapter also raises the issues encountered by women in responding to their abusive situations, the factors that finally led to some women separating and the effects on women and their children. Chapter 4 then examines professional and agency responses to abused disabled women through a discussion of the findings of the two national surveys, of the domestic violence and disability sectors, as well as the experiences women had of 'helping' professionals. Together, both chapters highlight the fact that, while disabled women experience complex and prolonged domestic violence and abuse, there is currently a severe shortage of services to assist them with their situations, made worse in turn by the general absence of effective responses from existing professionals and agencies.

Chapters 5 and 6 are contributed by Ruth Bashall and Brenda Ellis, both of whom are well-known disabled activists, practitioners and consultants in the UK who offer disability equality training and have worked on domestic violence and issues for disabled women for many years. Brenda was one of the advisors to the research which informs this book, and Ruth offered disability equality training to the non-disabled members of the research team and to Women's Aid managers as an integral part of the study. The research team was grateful for this invaluable assistance, which greatly facilitated the study. Brenda and Ruth not only contributed their expertise to the research overall and produced the two general chapters based on their activism and experience, but they also advised, edited and were involved in the book project throughout. These chapters discuss activism, understandings, policy and practice in relation to abused disabled women, with multiple illustrations from existing activist and service-providing projects.

In Chapter 7, we build on our discussions of abused disabled women's experiences to further consider the failings and gaps that exist in terms of services and identify what would constitute good practice, were it to exist. We present some examples of existing best practice and the chapter is written to assist practitioners and professionals in the field. Chapter 8 takes this analysis further, looking at the strategic framework in which services for disabled women experiencing domestic violence sit. We identify good practice in terms of strategic and commissioning guidance and funding regimes. Both these chapters include a bullet-pointed list of practice recommendations for ease of use by busy professionals. In the final chapter, we draw together the various threads and themes discussed throughout the book and the important issues for abused disabled women highlighted through our research.

Thus, in the next few chapters, we will discuss disabled women's experience of abuse, their advice to practitioners, and the responses of services available, but we will begin by looking at the background and the existing research on the issue. What, in more detail, does the research done so far (apart from our study) tell us about disabled women, their needs and the services available?

Chapter 2

What the Research Tells Us

A Story of Gaps and Failings

Lack of research evidence in the UK and internationally

The first thing the research literature tells us is that there is not very much of it in any country. Looking at studies that have been carried out, it quickly becomes clear that there has been very little research in the UK itself on domestic abuse and disabled women in either the domestic violence or disability arenas. Research is needed to support service and policy development in any field but, in this case, it has been thin on the ground, in fact almost non-existent until the first decade of the twenty-first century. The studies that do exist have been pioneering, but have been small-scale and conducted with scant resources.

Three small UK studies were conducted in the 1990s in Waltham Forest and Islington, both of which are in London (Hill 1995; James-Hanman 1994), and in Scotland (Macleod and Cosgrove 1995). In exploring abused disabled women's experiences of accessing service provision, all of these identified a catalogue of failures and inadequacies in existing provision. Other studies have not been specific to the subject. For example, in some studies of disabled women's lives, intimate partner violence has emerged as a theme, but only as one amongst many (Depoy, Gilson and Cramer 2003). McCarthy (2000) has conducted important work with women with learning difficulties but, until our study, there was no equivalent for women with physical and sensory impairments.

The earlier work was followed by a ground-breaking study in the early 2000s. Conducted in the Middlesbrough area by Jill Radford and her colleagues in response to the domestic homicide of a disabled woman, this study identified blockages faced by disabled women in situations of domestic violence in trying to get away from the abuse (Radford *et al.* 2006; Trotter *et al.* 2007). Further discussed later in this chapter, these blockages and difficulties make it very difficult for disabled women being abused to get the help they need.

Internationally, there is a wider range of research on which to draw, presenting findings from which researchers, activists and practitioners in the UK can learn. (For a selection of examples of this research, see Brownridge 2009; Chenoweth 1997; Dorian 2001; Garland-Thompson 2005; Martin *et al.* 2006; Nosek and Howland 1998; Nosek *et al.* 2001; Nosek, Hughes and Robinson-Whelan 2007.) In Australia, influential contributions by Lesley Chenoweth and her colleagues were among the first to demonstrate that disabled women are often so devalued that they are 'invisibilised' and perceived as asexual. Disabled women are often not seen as being 'proper' adult sexual women, which can expose them both to being infantilised and to grave risk of emotional, physical and sexual abuse. When such abuse happens, Chenoweth and her team found that disabled women are then likely to be overlooked by both disability and domestic violence support systems (Chenoweth 1997; Chenoweth and Cook 2001). Chenoweth has both developed theoretical understandings of disability and evaluated Australian national and state level responses in terms of domestic violence (see, for example, Chenoweth and Clements 2007).

Research exploring disabled women's experiences of abuse in North America has been similarly world-leading, with work by Margaret Nosek and her co-workers viewed by all commentators as of key importance (see, for example, Nosek, Howland and Young 1997; Nosek *et al.* 2001). Much of this work has revealed inadequate service provision in the United States, very similar to the findings in Australia and the UK. Going back to the 1990s, for example, Young *et al.* (1997) conducted nationwide, large-scale research revealing inadequate service provision across the board. Ongoing research since then has to date confirmed this lack of services, coupled with a higher incidence of domestic abuse among American disabled women compared with non-disabled women (Martin *et al.* 2006; Nosek *et al.* 2006).

In a further international example geared more towards activism and advocacy but including research too, the Canadian organisation of disabled women activists, DAWN, has a variety of branches in different cities, and works to promote the equality, rights, inclusion and empowerment of disabled women and girls through education, advocacy, coalition-building and publications (see www.dawn.thot.net). DAWN combines research with activist and practical initiatives to address the gaps in provision and to improve practice and societal attention to the issue.

Despite such good practice in some contexts, both internationally and nationally, there are further gaps in relation to diversity and equality in most countries where research has been done. Thus, the nature of the evidence available has been further limited by the fact that previous studies both in Britain and internationally have often failed to include the experiences of lesbians and of disabled women from black, minority ethnic and refugee (BMER) backgrounds (Begum 1992; Vernon 1997, 1998). A large-scale study in Western Australia (Cockram 2003) is one of the few that systematically includes the experiences of women from minority groups as a key component. Twenty per cent of participants were from diverse cultural heritages and a further 28 per cent from indigenous backgrounds, and their situations were usually significantly worse than those of majority white women. Another Australian study (in Victoria) found there had been some progress in incorporating women with disabilities into family violence reforms, but these changes were quite inadequate to the task, most particularly for women from indigenous and minority communities (Healey *et al.* 2008). Margaret Nosek and her colleagues also identified key psychosocial characteristics of abused women with physical disabilities, the majority of whom were from disadvantaged minority groups, in a 2006 study of disabled women in Texas (Nosek *et al.* 2006).

Isolation, vulnerability and issues of power

The seriousness of the gaps in existing knowledge and services is compounded by the consistent suggestion in the literature since the mid 1990s that, in general, disabled women may experience abuse in ways that non-disabled women do not (see, for example, Chenoweth 1997; Nosek *et al.* 2006; Sobsey 1994). Cockram's research (2003) showed that disabled women experience the same kinds of violence as other women, but that this is massively amplified by impairment-specific abuse.

Most particularly, abused disabled women experience additional difficulties in situations where they are reliant on their abusers, especially if these are also their partners and carers. Having to rely on abusive partners for personal assistance with daily, and perhaps personal, care tasks is likely to make disabled women even more vulnerable and unsafe (Nosek *et al.* 2001). The issue of control comes to the fore in this extremely painful personal context (Magowan 2003, 2004). What is someone who is a wheelchair user to do, for example, if their carer deliberately places their personal hygiene items or medicines out of reach, or refuses to provide them?

It can also be more difficult to find out if any help or support is available if you are dependent on your carer to assist you to contact the outside world or to go to the shops. A paper by Saxton and colleagues alludes searingly to this difficulty (Saxton *et al.* 2001). It is called 'Bring my scooter so I can leave you.' Finding out about support available, being able to access other people for help, and leaving an abusive relationship may thus be especially problematic for disabled women. Furthermore, sources of protection open to other women (for example, outreach centres) are often less accessible to disabled women and they may therefore be forced into the situation of having to endure abuse for longer before seeking help (Humphreys and Thiara 2002; James-Hanman 1994). There are further difficulties that disabled women may experience in leaving their home if, for example, it has been specially adapted for them with aids and facilities, or if a care package of home-based community care services has been organised (see Cross 1994, 1999), especially if the abuser was part of setting this up.

At the same time, if a disabled woman's abuser is also her carer, she may be particularly reluctant to see him (or her) arrested or otherwise removed. Women who do decide to leave are likely to have more complex needs, which may include accessible transport and accommodation, including refuge-based support, or help with personal care or sign language interpreters (see Nosek *et al.* 2001). Domestic violence support services may not be able to meet these various needs. Further, because of disabling social attitudes and lack of access or awareness, more general sources of assistance, such as criminal justice and legal remedies, are often less accessible to disabled women, increasing their possible isolation and vulnerability.

Perpetrators frequently appear to abuse their partners in ways which increase the powerfulness of their own situation, making use of and exploiting the woman's impairment or condition. For example, a small-scale, qualitative UK study by Magowan (2003, 2004) looked specifically at disabled women's experiences of abuse and explored how disabled women's increased vulnerability interacted with the mechanisms of abusive relationships to give rise to new types of violence and to more complex barriers to escape. Episodes and experiences of abuse were found to be intensified among disabled women, as compared with non-disabled women, and to be experienced over wider contexts and perpetrated by a greater number of significant others (Magowan 2004; Nosek *et al.* 1997). Magowan's study further suggests that more than 50 per cent of UK disabled women may have experienced domestic abuse during their lives (Magowan 2003). There are also some research indications (bearing in mind that studies have mainly been small-scale) to suggest that UK disabled women, regardless of age, sexuality, ethnicity or class, may be assaulted or raped at a rate at least twice that for non-disabled women (Chenoweth 1997; DAWN 1986; Magowan 2004; Sobsey 1994).

These findings are backed up on a larger scale by data from a sub-set drawn from the 1999 British Crime Survey (BCS), in which nearly twice as many disabled women, proportionally, were found to have experienced intimate violence compared with non-disabled women in the 16–29 years age bracket (Mirrlees-Black 1999). The 2006 BCS confirmed this, showing that having a limiting illness or disability was associated with an increased incidence of all types of intimate violence, inequality and vulnerability (Jansson *et al.* 2007). Similarly, an Australian 2000 survey indicated that 20 to 30 per cent of women experiencing sexual assault have some form of disability or special need, a far higher percentage than would be expected from disability population statistics (ABS 2004). Martin *et al.* (2006) also found, in a US study, that sexual assault was significantly increased for disabled women.

Where the woman's abuser is not her partner, there can still be very specific power and control issues. For example, the vulnerability, isolation and dependence which disabled women often experience are exacerbated when a paid personal assistant or carer is the perpetrator and may have a huge amount of power over the woman they are caring for in isolated, one-to-one situations (see, in an American context, Saxton *et al.* 2001). For example, Hassouneh-Phillips *et al.* (2005) identified maltreatment by US health care workers through practices which invalidated, discounted and physically or emotionally hurt disabled women in their care, in a way rarely noticed by the authorities. Little is known in terms of research findings about what strategies disabled women may use to manage such difficulties (Powers *et al.* 2002). Power issues between perpetrators and disabled women have also been found to be accentuated by societal attitudes to disability, by disbelief or voyeurism from agencies, family members and friends, and for older or frail women (Magowan 2004).

Conceptualising disability, inequality and multiple systems of oppression

This book is principally about practical responses and policy development, but a brief mention here of conceptual frameworks may be of help. Various authors have added to ideas about the social model of disability in terms of women's experiences, pointing out that gender has often been overlooked as a disability issue. From an activist perspective, for example, it has been well-documented that women's services and movements have in the past tended to ignore disabled women (see, for example, Chenoweth 1997; Fine and Asch 1988). A recent UK study has added to this in a contemporary vein, analysing the inadequacy of theorising about oppression, disability and domestic violence and about the failure of political movements, including both the disability equality and the women's movements, which frequently continue to marginalise abused disabled women (Nixon 2009).

There have been attempts to move beyond this situation and to theorise understandings of the 'embodiment' of women's impairment and the discrimination and possible abuse that they may therefore face, compounded by differences in ethnicity, culture, class and sexuality (Morris 1996; Vernon and Swain 2002). 'Gendering' disability (see in general: Smith and Hutchison 2006) has become a subject of academic scholarship, and has begun to conceptualise connections between disability and violence against women. For example, Mays (2006) has developed an explanation, drawn from disabled women's views, in which domestic violence was defined as being a strongly gendered and further disabling experience. The paper argued that feminist interpretations and disability conceptualisations, with the emphasis (between them) on gender relations, 'disablism' and poverty provide, if used together, an effective analytical tool for exploring the debilitating nature and consequences of violence against disabled women, despite the previous overlooking of the issue.

On a wider global level, a Special Edition of *Wagadu*, the journal of transnational women's studies, has developed intersecting gender and disability perspectives on globalisation and international policies regarding disabled women (Parekh 2007). These analyses build on intersectional approaches to understanding multiple systems of oppression similar to those developed by black feminists in the late 1980s and early 1990s in relation, then, to teasing out the interweaving impacts of racism and sexism (along with class and sexuality issues). These contributions also highlighted the relative lack of attention to women from black and minority communities within the women's movement of the time. Thus, there are similarities between the ways in which black women's issues and disabled women's experiences get overlooked, which draw attention to the need to use an intersectional analysis in the development of new understandings which inform the provision of services and programmes of training and awareness-raising for abused disabled women and for practitioners.

The concept of intersectionality (see Nixon 2009; Shakespeare 1998; Thiara and Gill 2010) alludes to intersecting social divisions and discrimination. Intersectionality, increasingly popular in contemporary analysis of difference and oppression (for example, racism, discrimination against women and heterosexism) provides a powerful tool in general for an exploration of the structural location within society of abused women (Crenshaw 1991; Yuval-Davis 2006). The work of some feminists is of note here, and furthers our understanding of the complex 'subjectivity' and material location of many disabled women along an axis of power and disadvantage (Nixon 2009; Thiara and Hague with Mullender 2011).

Radford *et al.* (2006) further propose the existence of a 'double stigma', and Vernon (1998) suggests 'compounded disadvantage' for disabled women from some minority communities, for example for some South Asian women (see also Vernon and Swain 2002), while Chenoweth (1997) speaks of 'simultaneous discrimination' to flag up similar issues. Drawing on some of this earlier work, Nixon has more recently coined the term 'compound oppressions' to refer to the intersection of disablism and other forms of oppression which 'has implications for both the complexity of disabled survivors' experiences of violence as well as for [the] recognition of the abuse of disabled women as a pressing social issue' (Nixon 2009, p.85). In practice, though, agencies often fail to grasp these intersections. In a book on violence against women in South Asian communities, the first of its type, Thiara and Gill (2010) discuss, for example, how professional responses to minority ethnic women provide multiple examples of negative responses that lack any developed understanding of intersectionality, frequently just 'adding on' issues, such as ethnicity and disability.

Developments in service provision and policy

As far as services and policy are concerned, as already noted, difficulties have been identified in service provision in many countries, but it is important also to say that there have been moves towards improvement. In Australia, for example, there has been only a small amount of research to date on the attempts by disabled women to seek help from agencies, but there have been recent attempts to improve practice, with attendant guidelines, policy development and evaluations (Chenoweth and Clements 2007; Cockram 2003). Similarly, in the US, studies find that domestic violence programmes are providing some services to disabled women but are faced with challenges stemming from limited funding, lack of physical space, and lack of training (Chang *et al.* 2004). In Britain, the small-scale research conducted up till now on practical responses by agencies has consistently revealed a distressing lack, within relevant UK agencies and inter-agency or strategic partnerships, of dedicated service and policy development for disabled women who experience abuse (James-Hanman 1994; Trotter *et al.* 2007). As a result, many domestic violence practitioners and support organisations have become increasingly aware of difficulties in meeting the needs of women coming to them for assistance.

These difficulties may be compounded by lack of awareness of domestic violence in many, if not most, disability organisations, despite the activities of disabled women activists. The study we have noted by Jill

Radford and colleagues (Radford *et al.* 2006; Trotter *et al.* 2007) has shown that, while many professionals and survivors of violence hope for greater service development in the future, currently they recognise both individual and agency limitations in making the connections between disability and domestic violence. Barriers to effective intervention, identified in Radford's study and a variety of others, include a low take-up of domestic violence services by abused, disabled women and low numbers of women disclosing abuse to disability organisations, failures of awareness-raising campaigns, and fear among disabled women that services will be unsupportive of women's personal issues and inappropriate places in which to address them (Magowan 2004; Radford *et al.* 2006). Due to shortage of resources or perhaps a lack of prioritising, many domestic violence support services and disability organisations may not be able to meet these various needs.

Disability activists on domestic violence have led the way in challenging this situation in various countries. Usually unrelated to formal research, key practical, training, policy and investigative work has been undertaken by Greater London Action on Disability (GLAD) which is unfortunately no longer in existence, and by Scope, the UK Disabled People's Council (UKDPC, formerly the British Council of Disabled People) and the UK Disability Forum Women's Committee. This Women's Committee previously developed a useful website, produced by disabled women activists and organisations, which is helpful to abused disabled women seeking support (see Ellis 1995; UK Disability Forum 2008). The website has not been updated but is still available. These organisations are discussed in detail in Chapter 5.

Disabled women consultants and trainers have also offered training and support services. Most of these training and policy developments and innovations, however, have been conducted, as indicated, without formalised research assistance or support. Vitally, some key organisations have started to develop good practice in this area. The Leeds City Council Domestic Violence Team, previously the Leeds Inter-Agency Project (LIAP) (see www.liap.org.uk), has conducted pioneering work developing good practice and both policy and strategic development at the local level in local authorities and across strategic partnerships.

Statutory adult social services now operate 'safeguarding adults' and 'vulnerable adults' polices and services, and domestic violence organisations have been attempting, in recent years, to make their services accessible, especially in newly built properties (see the Women's Aid website at www.womensaid.org.uk). Helplines and independent living centres can offer meaningful support in the UK and their key supportive role has also been confirmed in other countries, for example in the United States (see Swedlund and Nosek 2000). Overall, though, all the studies so far, in both the UK and elsewhere, find poor (though sometimes improving) service development. Replicating the UK studies, for instance, pioneering studies by Howe (2007) and Healey *et al.* (2008) in Victoria, Australia, draw attention to the lack of adequate Australian data and services on violence against women for disabled women. These studies confirm others in suggesting that service agency shortcomings need to be addressed widely, with the active participation of disabled women themselves and within a human rights approach, through improved data collection, increased services, cross-sectoral work and capacity building.

In summary, then, disabled women have been found often to experience greater hurt and damage at the hands of abusers than non-disabled women, and this is likely to be increased even more if they are frail, ill or immobilised. The more severe impacts of the abuse are also due to the frequently more protracted duration of abusive episodes, attacks and relationships for disabled women (see Magowan 2004), related to the paucity of appropriate and knowledgeable service provision. This situation can thus set up a vicious circle of abuse in which disabled women may become increasingly 'damaged' by intensified and extended abusive episodes and/or relationships, exacerbated by the lack of available help (Magowan 2004). These inadequacies in provision apply to all disabled victims of domestic abuse, though lesbians and others experiencing same-sex abuse may be even more isolated and vulnerable.

Overall, isolation, vulnerability and neglect are the issues emerging from all the studies to date in various countries for disabled women experiencing domestic violence. In the next chapter, we begin to discuss the contributions of our study to addressing these various issues and the gaps which we have identified in research conducted to date.

Chapter 3

Disabled Women's Experiences of Domestic Violence and Abuse

In the previous chapter, we argued that, despite considerable development in theory and practice in both the domestic violence and disability fields, the links between domestic violence and disabled women have been under-examined in the UK. Moreover, despite extensive literature on domestic violence in the UK, knowledge about disability and domestic violence remains fairly scarce, making it difficult not only to give 'voice' to abused disabled women but also to support service and policy development. Some recent work, as we have noted, has importantly exposed the barriers in help-seeking faced by disabled women affected by domestic violence (Radford *et al.* 2006) as well as the tendency of theorists and political movements, in both sectors, to reinforce the marginalisation of abused disabled women (Nixon 2009). This has added to the international body of knowledge, discussed in the last chapter, which has provided a crucial springboard for researchers and activists in the UK to highlight the issues for abused disabled women and the implications for policy and practice. Our national study provides further necessary insight, as elaborated in this chapter, into the lives and situations of disabled women who have lived with domestic violence. By drawing extensively on the accounts of abused disabled women interviewed for our study, and through bringing their voices into the foreground, this chapter discusses in detail disabled women's experiences of domestic violence and abuse. This chapter, and the next, are built on particularly comprehensive quotes using disabled women's own words.

We interviewed 30 women who were aged between 20 and 70 years, though the majority were aged between 31 and 50, with those aged between 41 and 50 years comprising around half of the interviewed women. Women had a range of impairments though a number also had multiple impairments.

Nineteen of the women had children. (Further details of the methodology are provided in the Appendix.)

Although disabled women, like non-disabled women, are vulnerable to the possibility of domestic violence and abuse, given their particular situations the nature of their abuse is likely to be more complex as they may be subjected to types of abuse to which non-disabled women are not. As the discussion below shows, our research findings resonated with many of those in existing UK and international research, as summarised in the previous chapter.

Multiple and complex abuse

As noted, a number of writers have argued that dominant definitions of domestic violence, understood as intimate partner violence, are unable to capture and represent its complexity in relation to disabled women's experiences (Nosek *et al.* 2001; Radford *et al.* 2006). More generally, there has been a shift in the UK in recent years towards framing these issues as violence against women and recognising the links between diverse forms of violence targeted at women (see Horvath and Kelly 2007; Nixon 2009; Thiara and Gill 2010). Given the complex and multiple nature of abuse experienced by disabled women, a number of the women in our study questioned prevailing definitions of domestic violence and saw it as far more pervasive and wide-ranging than intimate partner violence:

> I think that the domestic violence thing, in a way, kind of misleads disabled women because you always think of a man and a woman married or in a partnership. He hits her. But actually it's far more complex than that… it's big, it's so big and I think it's uncomfortable for non-disabled people to face up to.

The time period over which violence and abuse was experienced by disabled women in our study ranged from 1 to 22 years; the prolonged nature of such abuse is also identified by other researchers (Young *et al.* 1997). For severely disabled women who were dependent on care, the experience had sometimes been life-long:

> Severely disabled women are often quite abused, anyway, throughout their lives. And it's not obvious abuse, it's not violence particularly, it's kind of sometimes quite manipulative and that…because you have to receive care, you're quite passive and people can abuse that very easily. It's a very easy thing, to abuse. So I don't think it's that unusual, either.

This was also the case for those women who had experienced multiple abuse from a range of individuals and agencies. As discussed in the next chapter, once separation occurred, it often took women many years to deal with the ongoing emotional effects of the abuse they had experienced, especially if this was something for which they had received little support. Those who perpetrated abuse against disabled women were many and varied. They ranged from intimate (including same sex) partners, to paid carers, care agencies and family members. Those women whose dependency on others was high were especially likely to have experienced abuse from more than one abuser and said that some sort of abuse had been a part of their lives since becoming dependent. In some cases, women had been with more than one partner who had been abusive.

All of the 30 women spoke at length about physical abuse, sometimes extreme, as well as the accompanying emotional degradation and humiliation to which they were subjected. Almost 60 per cent had experienced combined physical, sexual and emotional abuse, while a third said they had experienced combined physical and emotional abuse. Among the events and incidents which they recounted were being pushed down stairs or across a room, having objects thrown at them, having a hand placed over their mouths while being held down and being spat at, having their heads banged on the floor repeatedly, being stabbed or strangled, being held down and stamped on, being kicked in the stomach and being dragged by the hair. For some interviewees, such abuse had resulted in severe injuries, including permanent damage to eyes and ears, disfigurement, loss of an arm, loss of babies, fractures, and severe cuts and bruises. Alongside the physical abuse, women spoke about being isolated from other people, being prevented from leaving the house, abusers threatening to take the children away or turning children against them, and abusers controlling everything they did and intruding into every facet of their lives, which left them with no privacy.

Being disabled significantly affected the abuse disabled women were subjected to and made it worse. Abusers commonly used women's impairments to perpetuate particular kinds of abuse, including ridicule and insults about the woman's condition. In relation to this, women's voices speak for themselves in the following series of quotes from our interviewees:

> It can be more subtle. It can just be bullying. It can just be being laughed at, being humiliated. I mean, I know abusers do that anyway but it's *another* thing to be humiliated about. And, I'm just thinking, if you had a classic man and a woman, man being the abuser, the woman's kind of personal integrity is always involved. But she doesn't expect him to wipe her bottom and she doesn't have to rely on him to feed her or do whatever… There's something else there.

At night times he'd be in the living room and I'd be in my bedroom and he'd shut the door on me so I couldn't call him for anything, so he wouldn't hear me. And if I wanted to, like, use the toilet or anything he'd tell me to just piss myself there and then. Now obviously, for me, if I was non-disabled I'd be able to get up and do it. I'd be able to find some way of doing that. I'd get up and use the toilet. I wouldn't have to rely on him. I could get up and open the door. It was awful…obviously it got worse because I wouldn't do any sexual things as well, be intimate with him at all. That was my only weapon really.

There was slapping on the face, chucking me out of the wheelchair. And he grabbed me round the neck. He did slam my food down a few times. Or, one time, he got so jealous when he was picking me up from a respite place because one of the carers that worked at the respite place give me a kiss on the cheek and a cuddle goodbye. All the way home he thumped my leg all the time, and my arm, as well as shouting at me all the time, telling me he was going to take me back to my mum's house.

One time, he actually took the battery out of this wheelchair I'm in now. He just unplugged it so I couldn't move and, if it wasn't for a mutual friend that came to the house, he wouldn't have plugged it back in. And I don't know how long I'd have been staying there with a dead battery. There was no one else that was supposed to be going round to the house… He'd make me wait for the toilet or he'll tut a lot or he'll say 'Oh god you have to do it again. Oh come on then, get it over and done with.' And shove me about sometimes. Push me about to get me there, to get to the toilet and what have you.

He would take my car and leave me stranded. Most able-bodied women could get out of the house or drive your own car. If you are disabled you might not be able to – I couldn't.

He was drinking and getting worse and worse, I had a Motability car, he would take it and disappear for days on end with it, leaving me stranded in the house, unable to get the shopping, etc. But you don't say anything as a disabled woman. I felt so ashamed that this was happening so I didn't tell anyone, didn't ask anyone for help. I'd just be stranded.

What he liked to do was to hold the chair down just as I was trying to move in it somewhere – with his hands on here, like this, so I couldn't move – or, this is a great one, move it away just as I was shifting myself into it…

Women's accounts clearly show that, given their dependence, their abuse experiences are complex and at times all-pervading. For women who had developed their impairment after being in the relationship, or where the impairment had worsened, the abuse also increased as the impairment/ condition worsened. Several of the women had not realised they were experiencing abuse, often because it started some time after they had been in the relationship and was so gradual and subtle that they had not recognised it until it escalated, became physical, and entered various aspects of their lives, or even until after separation:

> I didn't really get the abuse to begin with, I got it afterwards. When I thought about it, after leaving him and everything, I got it afterwards and then I thought, 'That's abuse, in a way.' It's all, like, shouting at me or just pushing me into doing things or telling me off. And that was the first abuse. Later on is when the physical abuse came in.

In a few cases, the abuse had started or escalated on the birth of a child or when the child was young:

> After giving birth to my second daughter…I noticed that my body was getting very very tired to the point where I could hardly walk. And, to do things for my daughter during the day and that, I was getting more and more reliant on other people. And he just didn't want to give me that… he didn't want to give me the support and help that I needed. If anything, he was putting more pressure on me. He had another child as well, from another relationship, who he wanted to come down…if anything he wanted me to take him on as well… And, anything that he did for me, he'd always make me know that he's done it.

Sexual violence was also commonly experienced by disabled women, something which many of them had never told anyone about until the interview. Disclosing was often a part of a process of beginning to deal with what had happened to them: 'She took away who I was really. I think that's really hard to explain to people. It's so shameful but you kind of stuff it all away.' Women interviewees gave numerous accounts of constant and unrelenting forced sex and repeated rape by partners and sometimes fathers, including sexual assaults in front of children. Women who had to maintain intimate relationships with abusers who also sexually violated them spoke about the tremendous strain this had placed on them:

> Yes, I was exhausted, absolutely exhausted, shattered. And being Deaf is hard work you know, you have to concentrate so much harder… And, as well as having two small children and having to go to work and, in the evenings, I'd be exhausted. And he'd be furious and slap me and kick me awake. And he used to say, 'Don't you fall asleep on me, I want a wife, a real wife not an old woman.' And, you know, it was sex all the time, twice a day and he would shout at me and then hold me down and I hated it, I hated it.

Abusive partner-carers: control not care

Given the dependence of disabled women on their partner-carers, the use of women's impairments as part of the abuse by partners compounds their abuse experiences and increases the difficulties faced by women, especially in relation to looking for help with their situations.

Deliberate neglect at the hands of both abusive partner-carers and other family members, with the resulting vulnerability, was commonly reported by women in our research. Being denied access to vital medicines which were withheld or put out of reach, or being deliberately deprived of sanitary protection, soap and personal washing items were some of the experiences shared by interviewees:

> He would use me being disabled. I felt useless because he wouldn't do anything for me and I'd be stuck. He would watch me get worse. I had a two-burner cooker on a trolley, he chucked it across the room and cut it up and then said, 'Now you try cooking something...'

Such neglect was compounded by the isolation imposed on women by their abusers. As shown by other research on domestic violence, isolating women from family, friends and other networks is a common abuse strategy adopted by many abusive partners (Radford *et al.* 2006). In our study, isolating a woman from other external carers was often a deliberate abuse strategy which increased women's isolation and created greater dependence, multiplying the effects of neglect:

> I suppose you don't even recognise it to start with. And I lived here with two of my live-in PAs [personal assistants] and then we got together and, I think, even then right at the beginning of our relationship, she was actually quite abusive. I just didn't really notice it. So things like, she would take money out of my purse without asking me and go down the pub, quite regularly. And, at the time, you think 'Oh never mind.' You just kind of skim over it and don't think about it...when she was drunk she was quite physically aggressive. She used to try and pull me out of my chair and do things like that. Leave me, whatever. And then there was a big fight between her and my two PAs that lived in at the time and they decided to leave.
>
> And then [partner] and me were on our own and I think that was kind of what she wanted really, the situation that she wanted. So she had free access to my bank account. She had free access to my van. She had free access to anything that I had, really. And it's really weird because, one of the times, I was sitting on the loo and I called her because I wanted to get off the loo. She came in and she said 'Well, now that the PAs have gone, I'm not going to be running around after you. So you'll have to wait.'

> So she would like leave me in situations like that quite regularly... She actually alienated everybody, even my sister who I've always been really close to.

Isolating strategies not only increased women's dependency but left them with little energy to maintain relationships with family and friends, which further served to compound their situations:

> You kind of don't want to see them any more, and they phone and you don't phone them back. And you become more and more isolated and almost stuck in the situation.

Over and over again, women's narratives highlight the intensity of their vulnerable situations, including extreme isolation, dependency on abusive partner-carers, and inability to leave, often in the face of few services and opportunities:

> Being disabled, well it just dominated it, the way he was able to treat me because of it... But he would go round and close the windows so the neighbours couldn't hear, he would take the phone and throw it out of my reach, grab my hair and drag me because he knew I couldn't do anything about it. And then plonk me on the stairs where I would be stuck, pin me down with his hand around my mouth.

> You see, there is two levels of isolation going on if you are disabled and abused, a double level and layer so you are more isolated in all sorts of ways.

> You know, the same opportunities are not there for Deaf or disabled people. We're forced to become dependent to a certain extent because the facilities aren't there. You don't want to add to it. You know, that awful dependence through no fault of their own, you know, because life is as it is and the opportunities are just not there. You don't have the educational opportunities that other people have, and training and job opportunities.

Impairment-specific abuse included being denied access to wheelchairs and other mobility aids, being left stranded for hours or days, and being prevented from accessing needed facilities. Women's accounts provide numerous examples of the ways in which abusive partner-carers reinforced women's dependence as a way of asserting and maintaining their control over women:

> He was the one that charged up the wheelchair. If he didn't charge it, it turned off and if he didn't charge up the wheelchair I couldn't move. Or he didn't help me in the hoist and get me into the chair. He helped me get dressed and helped me go to the toilet or whatever. I was completely reliant on him... But, I mean, it was like he was making me think I needed him here all the time.

Physically, he did make me worse. He made me a lot more reliant on him and he wanted me to rely on him to control me more. But…of course I'm reliant on some people, I can't help it, but I'm not as much as what he made me think. He really made me rely on him.

Because they become your carer and they make you believe that you need them because of your disability. And they do everything: 'And I'm making life so much easier for you.' You know, and I thought it was wonderful. Nobody had taken care of me in that way. No one. You know, and it was like, 'God, he'll do the ironing! He'll cook! He'll clean!' And bit by bit, though, he was taking everything. He was buying my clothes. He was telling me who I could see. Where I could go. I mean, part of that is about being a woman, but a lot of it was I couldn't get anywhere unless he took me. Non-disabled women don't have that problem. They can walk, he carried me out. He always made a thing about not pushing me out in my wheelchair. He'd carry me out to the car. Just to emphasise it more.

For those women who were able to leave the house on their own and access the outside world or who had shared what was happening with some friends, the effects of the abuse were somewhat reduced:

It [disability] has a lot of effect on it because it's difficult to get away from it. If I wasn't living in this town, I would possibly have lots of mental illness because my saving grace is that I can go out of this house and go down the town on my own, so it gets you away from the person that's there. And, I mean, it's quite frustrating when people come and they see the people who work for me because they all think they're extremely nice. But it's different visiting somebody and actually having to live with them. And it's only close friends that really understand.

The vulnerability described and felt by disabled women was often greater when they were subjected to physical abuse, even though they were not always passive:

He would take away the things I needed. I would say 'It takes two to tango. I know I am awkward but please don't hit me.' He'd say: 'You've got a mouth on you. You can't defend yourself, though, can you.' I was so vulnerable, just at his mercy.

She would kick me quite regularly. She was doing a martial arts course, doing karate. And so, if I was doing something she didn't want me to do, she would throw things around. She was always breaking telephones and broke the TV once… I mean, she'd take my mobile phone off me and then quite deliberately verbally abuse me and then physically kick me. But she'd strangle, go to strangle me. I'd be arguing, I wouldn't, like, necessarily just be passively taking it. I would be shouting back, often. But it would then become quite physical.

> I would try to placate him and say 'Don't hurt me.' Because I was disabled I knew he could hurt me easily, you see.

Women spoke at length not only about the physical dependence on abusive partner-carers but the emotional degradation, associated with the impairment, to which they were subjected. The following words of a woman in her fifties were typical of many made by the women in our study:

> He'd insult me with all those names, 'You spazzy' and so on. 'Who'd want to marry you? Just look at you...' Shouting insults, 'You cripple,' all that sort of thing. Once, when he was furious, he threw me on the floor with my dinner and said, 'That's where you eat your dinner. That's where you belong.' Of course I couldn't get up again.

Financial abuse and control, as can be seen from some of the above accounts, was also a common occurrence for women who found themselves in situations where abusive partner-carers took control over benefits and finances or denied them money, sometimes for necessary prescription medication or for essential personal needs related to the impairment. Some women spoke about having to live off child benefit, while their partners who were well paid subjected them to severe financial abuse. In a few situations, women's abusers had gained total control over their finances, sometimes using this to fund alcohol and/or drug dependency. In one case, a woman with an extremely painful condition was made to sleep on the floor because her partner would not spend money on buying her a bed. For another woman, developing a disability had led to her husband and his family conspiring to get rid of her after she could no longer work:

> He and the whole family caused arguments. They threw me out one December. When I fell ill, they blamed me because they wanted me to go to work and get money.

Such physical and financial dependence, coupled with isolation, often made it virtually impossible for women to look for help. Further, when the abuse was dressed up as 'caring' and used to exert greater power and control, this made it difficult for women to 'name' abuse and to do anything about it, and was a situation where agencies were sometimes collusive:

> I didn't notice it...he loved doing things for me... I'd never been taken care of properly... It was all about caring and it was subtle. It was so subtle I didn't notice it until it had got to a degree of critical... [Also] I was in the process of getting [daughter] back [from social services]. I noticed through social services that they left me alone because he was around.

The representation of abusive partner-carers as 'caring heroes', where they portrayed themselves as having a hard time because of having to perform caring tasks and often had the sympathy of others even when they had got rid of other carers, combined with the dominant construction of disabled women as asexual, resulted in a number of the interviewed women believing, and being made to feel, that they were undeserving of a relationship and should be grateful 'for somebody there to look after me although he didn't.' This sometimes created dilemmas for women in doing anything about their abusive situations:

> ...your heart goes out to your partner because they are doing all your care work. And I do appreciate that...because some of it's quite physical and some of it's hard work. But, also, this was their home, I paid them so I was the money as well. And, to end all of that for one person, it sounds really awful. Can I kick them out of the house, make them lose their job and their relationship all in one go? So it's really harsh...and that was one of the things that always held me back, was that I couldn't really kick them out of the house because you wouldn't just lose your house, you would lose your job and our relationship and all the things that go with those.

Feeling unworthy often made women feel ashamed to tell family and friends about the domestic violence and abuse, as well as there being pressure on them to tolerate abuse because 'who else will look after you?':

> People pity him because he is taking care of you... People are reluctant to criticise this saint or to think he could be doing these terrible things. And possibly, as well...people don't really 'see' a disabled woman as a wife, partner, mother. So I think for some people it's hard to think, well, this might be a woman who's being sexually or physically abused by her partner, is experiencing domestic violence, because disabled women don't have sex, do they?

Alongside the absence of appropriate services they could access for help, disabled women in same-sex relationships were also disbelieved about their abuse experiences:

> Because you can't run away from it. It's not like I could have gone to a safe house or anything like that – they don't have hoists. They wouldn't understand the PA system. You know, the whole system just wouldn't work. And, as well, it was a woman abusing me. Which people don't really see as abuse...people still laugh if I say 'Oh yeah, she was really abusive.'

Women's experiences also revealed that those who had been subjected to verbal and mental abuse, however great, had received less positive responses because control issues and threats to harm were not taken as seriously in their cases as they were for those who had been physically abused. Our interviewees believed this also to be part and parcel of the view of disabled women as asexual, women who should not be in intimate partnerships:

Your pride's at stake... Look, here's somebody who wants to be with me and then, over a period of time, it deteriorates and you don't want to say to people 'I'm scared', you know, 'I don't know what to do about it?'... I think, definitely, for disabled women that there is this issue of, like, 'Oh you're so lucky that you've got somebody' that you think, 'I'm not going to get somebody again. I'd rather put up with this'...because there is some nice times and, you know, he is sorry. So this is better than being on my own.

Yes, it was horrible, it just used to make me cry and cry, all because of being disabled. He would call me names and say I was stupid and that he was embarrassed to be seen out with me. As a disabled woman, there is a reluctance to ask for help, you know. You're embarrassed and you know people are already giving you lots of support. You don't want to add to it. You don't want to become even a bigger burden.

The terror of living with an abusive partner-carer on whom they were totally dependent was a reality for many of the women in our study and created huge contradictions in terms of issues of care and control, as highlighted by this woman:

He was killing with kindness. If it wasn't kindness, he was booting me in the stomach so no one could see the bruises. He learnt that pretty fast. Physically, I suffered...and all those things about when the phone rings and you just stop, or a car would pull up outside and I would just be frozen. You have that moment of absolute terror that it's them...which is quite hard when you need someone as well.

Where a woman regained some power by moving into accessible accommodation, ironically this could make the abuse worse:

My consultant thought a lot of my problems were because the flat we were in was inaccessible to me and I had to depend a lot on him for that. And a purpose [designed] bungalow with 24-hour care on site would be ideal. That's when my real problems started because I was given power back. The manager of the site was saying to my ex-husband, 'You don't need to do that any more, we're here to do the ironing and the cleaning. We're here to take the pressure off you.' He wasn't going to have any of it but, then, he didn't really have a leg to stand on because I had something that was concrete to say, 'Well you're always complaining it's too much ironing, there's too much washing, you can't keep up with everything.' So I said to the manager in front of him, 'Yeah I do. I want two hours ironing a week and I want...' That's when the beatings got worse. They suddenly became not two years, they became every other day, depending on how much I exerted my personality or demands.

Abuse by paid carers

Abuse from paid carers, considered widespread and common in disabled women's lives by our interviewees, had certainly been a reality for some of them, though professional understanding of both the relationship of disabled women with paid carers and the nature of the abuse perpetrated by them was seen to be limited (Saxton *et al.* 2001). In particular, issues were raised about the lack of attention given to mental and financial abuse, abusive invasions of privacy, and the control exerted by paid carers over disabled women. These were reported sometimes to be pervasive and continual, but are seldom acknowledged in definitions of abuse or by agencies. The abuse experienced by disabled women from paid carers was especially hidden as it was often non-physical:

> I think that all abusive relationships can be very psychological but I do think that it seems to be more psychological because it's a lot more subtle and it's very very hard to prove. Whereas, if you've been…if there's been a violent attack on somebody, you'd usually have the scars to show it. But when it's not that form of abuse, how do you prove it? How do you get people to take you seriously?

> Well, I have been stolen from and abused by my care workers, and then there was a huge argument with social services and the housing people because they refused to believe it or even investigate it. They were just on the care workers' side and got serious and judgemental if I started to try to tell them about it.

Having their privacy eroded by paid carers and the general intrusion into their lives was an aspect of abuse against disabled women that was poorly understood and that generally receives little attention:

> [It] can be quite abusive when people don't respect that [privacy] and they think they should be privy to everything that you do in your life. If you buy something new and they see it in the wardrobe. 'Oh I've not seen that before,' you know. Listening in to phone calls and knowing too much about your finances. That abuse of power is a big thing.

> If you want anything to be kept without anybody looking at it, you've really got to lock it up. Because I made a list of things for a new PA that was coming to work for me, I left it on there and the PA that was there said, 'Oh I see you've got a lot of things on the list for her to do.' And I'm thinking to myself, 'Well why did you turn it over and read it,' you know… they might sound very petty things, but they are a form of abuse really.

I was in a non-sexual relationship with this man and she was very jealous because she had a bad relationship with her husband and she didn't like me being with this man. She'd never really got anything good to say about him.

Women who directly employed paid carers spoke about the difficulty of critiquing poor practice while being dependent on them for care:

It's quite a difficult one to explain, really, but it's extremely difficult to act as an employer and discipline people in this position. When in the next moment you might have to ask them to do some very intimate task for you. So, basically, once you've got somebody working for you, you're more or less stuck with them because most people who do this don't do disciplinaries because they're frightened to do them.

This was further exacerbated when collusion between care workers and agencies led to the increased marginalisation of disabled women:

Because there's a lot of relationships between the agencies and you can be left out in the cold. They talk without you and decide what they think and, if you are disabled, you have even less say. So they [social services and housing association] were just laughing with the care workers behind my back. What I said didn't count.

I was not so much exploited by them as by the whole system. If you complained about the PAs, not only were you in trouble with them, you were in trouble with the housing association, social services. So they'd say, 'Why are you refusing care?' You know as if I'd done something wrong... And it is to do with them all being private now. There are less controls and the wages are bad, so they get different people and there are less checks.

Women interviewees had experienced great difficulty, in the face of little or no available support for disabled women around such issues, when taking action against paid carers or asking them to leave. Although the self-directed support programme and personalisation agenda, which extend the provision of direct payments, give women greater control over who to employ, the absence of adequate professional support – peer support being often all that is available – led to much anxiety and a fear among disabled women in this situation of having their funding cut back. They frequently felt that, as the system of provision of direct payments requires an independent living review every year, any problems with the care they had received could rebound unless they were seen really to need the care and to be clearly grateful for it.

Women responding to the abuse

Women interviewed in the study had responded to the abuse they had experienced in a wide variety of ways, as illustrated in the following series of direct quotes:

> It affected it a lot, did being disabled, because 'How to respond?' I couldn't really do anything and I needed him here to take me to the toilet, to put me to bed or whatever, or get me up in the morning. He needed to be here at certain times, otherwise I'm stuffed basically. So he knew he had to be.

> You can't fight back because, like, I can't walk out. So, when it happened… sort of, say, like an able-bodied person would just get up and walk out or what have you. But I couldn't. The only time I could get away from it was when I was in bed, he didn't come into bed with me.

> Well, one way it made it worse was, like, it was hard for me to talk to other people and hard to be understood and, like, I would just feel so pathetic. Like I was going to be pitied and I was pathetic anyway because of not hearing and speaking like other people. And in getting away – well I didn't feel I could for a while because I was so used to him and us going out together and it could be hard to call for help, I'd feel stupid and my voice would come out funny if I called out and people might laugh and not realise so I would keep quiet…

> Yes, it makes it worse because you can't physically get away. For example, on the night he got picked up for drunk driving, I was on crutches. I tried to defend myself, he took a crutch and broke it across his knee and said, 'You're next…' Without the crutch, I couldn't move away…I was in a helpless position.

Every single woman we interviewed recognised that being disabled made the abuse worse and limited their capacity to get away from the abusive situation or to respond to it in other ways. Women spoke about their inability to see or hear an attack, to move after an attack – to escape – and the lack of training and jobs for disabled women. Given their limited options, women who had no recourse to public funds were especially caught in the abusive situation even where they had attempted to leave; not being able to speak English also exacerbated this situation. Without funding, they could not access the support services they required:

> I got the number of a refuge from somebody at work but, when I rang them, they said they couldn't help because I had no indefinite leave [to remain].

Clearly, as the foregoing discussion shows, disabled women's reasons for being in, and staying in, abusive situations were complex and the barriers they encountered led to them staying in abuse for longer periods:

> I would imagine that they put up with it longer than women without disabilities because we find it more difficult, statistically and every way, to have a partner. We find it more difficult to have a supportive partner who knows the difference between being a carer and a controller. I mean, I can't speak for all the people with disabilities, but I think some see us as sort of children and all think we're women that need looking after a bit more. And those are the men that are more likely to become controlling and take it too far, you know…we're very cautious about men and their motives and why they want to be with us.

For a wide range of reasons, and as elaborated further in the next chapter, many women in our research had not told anybody about the abuse for long periods, if ever, before the interview. This was especially the case for those women who had developed an impairment later in life and those who had children:

> I didn't tell anybody. I kept it to myself really. I just tried to make things as pleasant and as normal and happy as possible in my own home. Especially like so the youngest one wasn't affected by it. If anything I was probably hiding it really.

Shame, guilt and self-blame were commonly experienced by our interviewees. Blaming the woman for the abuse was something which, in many cases, was reinforced constantly by the abuser, making it much more difficult for her to seek help:

> I think I was just ashamed, really… In the beginning, I thought it was my stupid fault. What did I do to deserve this and it must have been my fault. And the way he was saying it as well. He was saying that it must be, 'Go and think about what you've done wrong.' So he sort of told me I was wrong and it was me. So I thought it was all me in the beginning.

As already noted, some women did not recognise what was happening to them as domestic violence and abuse at the time, with this being a prime reason for not disclosing it to anybody or doing anything about it. Some later recognised that they were probably in denial at the time:

> I wasn't fully aware of it, really. I was just trying to make the best for all… making excuses, really. Denying it, if anything.

For some women, the prospect of being with an abusive partner was preferable to 'a life of care agencies' and this had led to them staying in the abusive situation for many years. Thus, having to receive care from agencies, or being placed in care homes and being institutionalised, were often very real fears, and shaped their responses to their abusive situations.

Why women left or separated

> But he grabbed my wrists and he held me on the bed [crying] and grabbed my arms and got me to sign paperwork [crying]… And eventually he pushed me up against the wall. Both my daughters were in the house. And the eldest one turned the music up full blast and the youngest in her bedroom next door hid underneath the duvet cover. And it was after that I knew that I'd got to do something.

> [He] was driving me around these roundabouts, screaming at me. I was nearly falling out of my chair. I was strapped in, but I was nearly falling out. And I kind of said, 'Well that's it.' I think I was really scared that we were going to have a car accident, actually. And I said, 'Well that's it. It's over. It's finished.' I started laughing. I don't know, at that point something in me just kind of…this calmness came over me. And it was like, 'No sorry, you've got to go. I've had enough. It's too much. You're going to kill me.'

> He became really abusive, verbally abusive to me. He was really screaming at me, 'You didn't tell me. You always forget these things.' It's all, like, using my disability against me… And just him saying that, I just thought, 'I can't do this no more.' I think it was something that clicked, that just sort of said, 'You've got to get out of here. You can't do this no more.' And I thought, 'Well how am I going to do that because he's in here.' And I thought, 'Right, come on. What do you need? You've got a coat,' and I got a coat, and I got a lead for the dog, and opened the door and went out.

All of the women in our study had separated from abusive partners or were no longer in a situation of abuse. Most of the women spoke about the 'triggers' that had led to their making the decision to leave or separate from those abusing them. In these cases, as illustrated above, all spoke about the moment that they realised it had to end. Having access to a supportive organisation, becoming more confident, and escalation in abuse to the point where women believed they would be killed were the factors that led women to make the decision to leave:

> But at the end, when I did actually go, he tried to strangle me with a telephone wire and raped me at the same time. And I passed out. He thought he'd killed me. But if I hadn't have passed out he probably would have because I think he would have carried on. And, as always, very remorseful because I think it scared him that he could actually kill me. And I took that cue to get out. I had to leave my children. I didn't know I

could take them with me. If I'd have tried to take them as well he would have got suspicious.

The weight was just dropping off me. I knew that I'd made that decision and I'd got to go with it. There was no sort of 'Shall I, shan't I?' I had a feeling that, when he came back this time, that was going to be it. I really did think he'd kill me.

Several women had left because of their children:

And then it got to the point where I used to get him arrested and taken from the house because he would start crashing things about. [My daughter] never saw any of it because she was either away at nursery, with friends, with Mum and Dad. I always had an inkling, I knew when it was going to go off and I knew when he'd start drinking and I'd get her out immediately. And, when I finally sort of split up, it was because I was reading her a bedtime story, it was half past eight in the evening, and he came in and he was drunk and he [was verbally abusive in front of her].

Even where women interviewed had psychologically and emotionally made the decision to leave, it took them many years to separate. Believing they had nowhere to go, support services being absent and the abuser's threats of suicide were typical of the factors that made women stay longer. Once an abuser left, women spoke about the relief this gave them:

Afterwards I slept and slept and slept like I've never slept before. I could sleep for, like, 24 hours in one go. Just absolute exhaustion. After that I started to sleep soundly again.

Interviewees also described feeling stronger and different after leaving abuse:

It's weird, when I left him… I know it sounds really strange but it's almost like a big weight had just lifted off my head when I got out of the house. And I felt stronger. I mean, I really did break down when I went round to see my neighbour and my brother and I really were crying. But, when I came round a bit more, I did feel stronger. And I felt, I can do this now and I've got to do it because I've got the backing of me brother and me mum pushing me to go do it and get my house back. And they all knew what had happened because of the statement I gave to me solicitor.

However, for several women separation did not mean the end of abuse; they continued to be subjected to post-separation abuse for some time, ranging from six months to four years. Post-separation abuse that disabled women were subjected to included continuous phone calls, abusive phone messages, turning up unexpectedly, stealing much-loved pets, and harassing family members:

He used to make phone calls at three o'clock in the morning to wake the household up. He used to write very nasty letters at least…well, I suppose, every other day I used to get a letter.

Sometimes post-separation violence was more unremitting for disabled women because it was harder for them to leave the area where they accessed services or had an adapted home and so they were more likely to encounter perpetrators even after separation.

How abuse affected women

I suppose he felt a bit trapped by me and then he started insulting me. He would make fun of how I speak and say I smelled which I don't, I know. And I would feel so hurt and humiliated. It was my first major relationship. It put me off, I felt that I couldn't be good enough to have relationships after that.

It had a massive impact on me. I lost who I was, my identity really. He left me with some things and, up to this day, I can't get them out of my head… I feel not very good about myself in that sense. And I feel that can be just as bad, even worse than being physically abused.

He'd go to the pub and come back in hopeless frustration. He called me a useless piece of shit and stuff like that. When I had just had the accident – I was incapacitated – I tended to agree and I felt worthless.

I became depressed and used to cry a lot because of the violence. I couldn't tell the midwife because of language. Now he's telling the court I'm mad, to get my daughter.

Clearly, their abuse experiences affected our interviewees in different ways and the structural barriers commonly faced by disabled women also accentuated the personal and psychological impacts of the abuse. Some women recounted at length how they had become severely depressed, lost a sense of self, begun to doubt themselves, saw themselves as unworthy of a relationship and generally felt worthless. Overall, abused disabled women struggled to maintain a positive self-image because of the intense emotional abuse which they almost always experienced:

When I remember emotional stuff, that is what I remember, 'You are a useless piece of shit'…it stays with me… Power of that mustn't be underestimated. If you're disabled, it's such a struggle to maintain a positive body image anyway, certainly I didn't – probably I thought that was all I was worth physically. I was impaired, I wasn't worth treating well and so on… Don't believe that any more… You can say you are as good as anyone who is non-disabled, but no use unless you actually believe it. Saying it is one thing, believing it is quite another. You almost think you deserve it.

Women who had experienced abuse from their paid carers found themselves not being able to trust anybody:

It's probably made me very cynical about why people go into this line of work. I think it can damage all other relationships if you're not careful, outside of the PA relationship, because you look for ulterior motives as to why people might want to relate to you.

When abuse was gradual and subtle and perpetrated by abusive partner-carers, interviewees spoke in detail about its profound and pervasive impact:

But the verbal abuse was so…difficult, so deeply undermining. I mean, I thought, 'At least he's not beating me to pulp,' but then you just feel worse and worse about yourself.

Dealing with the effects of multiple and lengthy abuse had taken several of the women a long time, either because they had never had any support and tried to come to terms with it themselves, or because it had been so pervasive that it had taken them years to move on: 'All I do is struggle and fight and keep on going…keep going… And it's like I'm tired.' A woman who had lived with severe depression and eating disorders had needed a great deal of support to deal with sexual abuse from her father, having buried it in her mind, when the same thing happened to her son who was raped by his father. In such cases, women were not only dealing with the impact of a legacy of lifetime abuse, but were having to deal with the impact of abuse on their children as well, as discussed below. A number of the women spoke about being depressed and a few women had developed eating disorders while some had problems sleeping:

He took everything. He took my complete independence where I had to ask him a fortnight before I needed sanitary towels to make sure that I'd get them. Like, one time, I ended up with too many because…I was so underweight my periods were irregular anyway. I only weighed four stone nine for ten years while I was with him.

Living in fear was also something that women said was an ongoing issue for them even after many years of separation, and especially where women had children:

To this day I think he's going to turn up. It'll never go, it won't go until I know he's dead.

I've got a thing about not going to sleep, because you've got to be awake, you've got to be on your guard. And I suppose I've never got over that. I can't get comfortable at night.

Children

Having children had often raised additional issues (see Mullender and Morley 1994; Mullender *et al.* 2002), though these varied for different women. Some stayed because of their children, while others left because of their concerns about the possible effects of the abuse on the children. For some women, the abuse started or increased when children were born or when they were small as they were often unable to look after them on their own and needed greater support from their partners or family members. Those women with children of an age to be aware of what was happening felt that the children had been negatively affected by the abuse. At times, children were used by abusers in the perpetration of abuse against women. At a time when they had minimal support in terms of care, some women felt frustrated at not being able to adequately care for their children who had to assume greater responsibility in the house. For some older children who carried out caring tasks for their mothers, the abuser disapproved of this support for the woman, and the situation created obvious problems:

Well, my eldest daughter, the relationship between her and my partner was just disrespectful, really. And there was a lot of tension…because she was obviously doing things for me at that point. Me mum stepped in and started helping me out in the home and helping me to get ready. And her little sister, they started doing more stuff in the house…he was there and he was criticising instead of helping. And me eldest daughter just didn't like that because she was doing it for me. She made it quite clear she was doing it for me and her younger sister, not for him. It was that kind of relationship.

Where women were greatly impacted by the abuse, children had grown up with great anxiety, often thinking that their mother would die.

Some women strongly believed that their impairment had been used against them by professionals in dealings about their children, and they had often felt pressurised by social and adult services. For one woman with high support needs, having children had meant that she had to fight with social services when her children were taken into care. Being able to show that she was in a relationship, albeit abusive, had assisted another woman in getting her children back. For another, her daughter was almost taken into care because there were no facilities for the woman. In a further case, a woman's husband and his family had colluded to keep her baby daughter when she was forcibly made to leave because of becoming disabled. Another husband had manipulated the children to such an extent that they stayed with him, despite previously wishing to be with their mother. Those interviewees who had to leave because their lives were in danger had left alone, not knowing they could take the children with them or that the accommodation they were going to would be able to house their children as well as themselves. One child of three years old was left with a violent father when the mother fled, and children's social services and others said nothing could be done and refused to help her get him back. This woman believed it would have been different if she had not been disabled.

Some children had been subjected to direct abuse, at times both physical and sexual. In a couple of cases, women reported their children being sexually abused by the same perpetrator as themselves. One woman's son was severely physically abused by his father for some time before she was able to have him back.

Where children continued to have contact with their fathers after separation, some women spoke about the children being influenced and used to undermine them as a way of abusers continuing the abuse – 'Surely but slowly he was using her to get at me as well. She's still quite nervous around him.' In such situations, children were frequently manipulated to participate in the abuse and turned against women by abusers:

> I mean, mentally, I knew he was doing a lot of damage to my son by saying that I was no good, I was a slag, I preferred other men to him.

Women had not realised until later the damage that living with and/or directly experiencing abuse had done to their children. At the time, they had believed that living with their father was the right thing for the children or had been so focused on getting through the day that they had had little space to consider the effects:

> To be honest, I didn't think about the impact on them because, it's like I said, you spend your life getting up and getting through that day and 'I'll make sure I don't do this, so this doesn't happen. I'll make sure I won't do that so he won't go off his head.' You know, it was like a cat and mouse game. And yet, the worst thing of all, I stayed because I didn't want them to lose their father. I was brought up on 'You should have two parents.' So it was all that as well. It was the fact that I wasn't going to deprive my children of a father, I was also terrified they'd be taken away from me again... And I realised, years later, that was the hold he had over me because it had already happened once. And the reason for that is, when they lifted the supervision order, they had my ex-husband swear

on the Bible to take care of us and that, to me, is sick. What message did that give him? What message did it give me? That was a very powerful message, to say 'You're so lucky.'

Indeed, many women reported 'containing things' to minimise the impact on their children, believing their children were okay if they did not see the abuse – 'In my mind everything was okay because my children didn't see it. I forgot about the hearing. The honest to god truth is I really didn't know of how it affected my children until I did this course.' Subsequently, many women had never looked for any help for their children, frequently because they did not know where to go. In a few cases, help for children was explored after separation, in the form of counselling and sometimes more creative channels:

> My youngest when he eventually left, I ended up seeking counselling help for her because there was a few things going on. She was being bullied at school as well and having to deal with her dad leaving…after she decided she didn't want it anymore we explored different ways to express what was going on for her. So she went into drama. Even when she didn't really want to do it, I kind of would say, 'No, you've got to try your best. Try your best.' She loves it now and, eventually, bits came out of how she felt about it all.

Conclusion

While many relationships between disabled women and partner-carers are, of course, not violent, those that are abusive are often distressing in the extreme, as this chapter has demonstrated. It is also the case that caring can be stressful and very difficult for the carer. But such frustrations are of a different order to the ongoing and serious abuse we have discussed here.

Disabled women's narratives have illustrated that their abuse experiences are often complex, extreme and sometimes prolonged, and may differ from those of non-disabled women because abuse is so closely linked to their impairments. Thus, disabled women's situations create greater vulnerability because of the intersection of gender and disability, which often makes women invisible and marginal, restricts their exit routes because of the absence of support services and other opportunities, and intensifies the effects on their sense of self because of systematic degradation linked to their impairments. Their location in society as 'disabled women' – marked by issues of gender, 'race'/ethnicity, age and sexuality – commonly influenced their subjectivity in our study and also dictated the responses they received from helping professionals and agencies, as discussed in the next chapter.

Chapter 4

Professional Responses to Disabled Women Affected by Domestic Violence

In the previous chapter, we outlined in detail women's experiences of domestic violence and abuse and the ways in which abusive partner-carers exploited women's impairments in their perpetration of abuse. As can be seen from their narratives, disabled women often believed they had few routes out of the abusive situation when they were living with the abuse. In this chapter, we focus on women's help-seeking and on professional responses to disabled women affected by domestic violence to further explore the central argument of this book, which is that issues of domestic violence and disabled women have been marginalised both by domestic violence services and disability organisations as well as inadequately responded to by the raft of other professionals women encounter.

This chapter draws on the two national surveys – of domestic violence services and disability organisations – conducted as part of the national study along with interviews with disabled women that explored their experiences with domestic violence services, disability organisations and other agencies and professionals. It is clearly evident from the findings that, while disabled women require greater and more complex service responses, commonly professionals and agencies continue to meet their needs inadequately, leaving many disabled women unprotected and in vulnerable situations.

National surveys

Two national surveys – of domestic violence services and of disability organisations – were conducted to establish the nature of services available to disabled women within both sectors. The survey of domestic violence services was sent, with the help of Women's Aid, to all domestic violence organisations in England (n=342) offering refuge, outreach and other forms of support to women experiencing domestic violence. These organisations were identified through Women's Aid lists and UK Refuges Online (UKROL).[1] A total of 133 responses to this survey were received, giving a response rate of 40 per cent. Simultaneously, by drawing on lists compiled by the UK Disabled People's Council and other national and local organisations, 348 surveys were sent out to disability organisations (of which no fewer than 26 closed for funding reasons during the survey process). A total of 126 responses were received, giving a response rate of 39 per cent, of which 53 simply said they did no work in this area, leaving substantive responses from only 73 organisations. Nevertheless, the national surveys provide an insight into the ways in which both the domestic violence and disability sectors are responding to issues of disability and domestic violence. The key findings from each are discussed here to provide an indication of what is offered by both sectors to disabled women experiencing domestic violence and the gaps that remain within domestic violence and disability services.

Domestic violence services

Available Women's Aid statistics provide an indication of the numbers of disabled women using domestic violence services. In 2006, Women's Aid and specialist domestic violence organisations in the UK provided services of different types to 131,245 women and 95,960 children in England. Women and children accessing refuge-based services numbered 16,815 and 19,450 respectively. Of these women, extrapolation from the annual Women's Aid Census Day figures[2] revealed that approximately 1170 were disabled women with physical and sensory impairments, giving a figure of 7 per cent. The survey further showed that 87 per cent of domestic violence organisations monitored referrals to them of disabled women, while 70 per cent routinely asked questions about disability to each woman being referred in order to best assist her. Some that did not do so were led by what women wished to disclose, some lacked the time to monitor, and others stressed that they provided a universal service to all women. However, good practice suggests that routine enquiry and the monitoring of services for numbers of disabled women using them (and explaining to women why this is being done) are the only ways to collect accurate information to assess need.

At the time of our research, 99 per cent of domestic violence organisations had equal opportunity policies, but only 87 per cent included disability, an anomaly which may have been addressed since then, given the requirement to include disability within such policies under the Equality Act 2010. The survey revealed that some form of specialist services to disabled women were offered by 38 per cent of organisations, though these were primarily 'structural' (for example, the provision of accessible accommodation, accessible transport, ramps or handrails) as opposed to 'attitudinal' (disability equality training), although a few refuges were able to offer specialised emotional support.

Although 94 per cent of domestic violence services were aware of disability legislation and were making attempts to meet it in terms of the accessibility of their properties, 76 per cent were not yet compliant. Some projects had specially adapted accommodation or facilities, and a few new-build properties offered clear examples of best practice in meeting disabled women's needs, providing fully accessible housing (for example, a whole adapted apartment). A wide range of adaptations were also provided, though most of these were in a minority of projects. Accessibility is also dependent on the ability to access personal assistance if necessary. Disabled women leaving their home area for a refuge may lose their care packages and hence their personal assistants or paid carers. Only around 13 per cent of refuges could provide, or otherwise access, temporary personal assistants (PAs) to assist disabled women staying at their projects. Several could offer accommodation to an existing PA who was able and willing to accompany a disabled woman to a refuge, although this would be expected to happen only rarely. Overall, though Women's Aid and other domestic violence organisations have improved their services in recent years, it was evident that accessibility remained a severe problem in many localities for disabled women seeking refuge.

While some structural changes had clearly taken place within domestic violence services, this was far less clear in relation to attitudes, even though these often underpin the impetus for social and organisational change. A number of responses did indicate awareness of the issues and an understanding of disabled women's experiences of domestic violence. Several projects gave accounts of the support they offered, the isolation and vulnerability of abused disabled women that they addressed, and the way in which their counselling and support services attempted to meet the needs of traumatised disabled survivors of abuse. A few had clearly taken on the issue in a whole-hearted way and were refreshing examples of good practice but, in relation to direct services for disabled women, the percentage of projects which could provide this was very low. Just over a quarter (27%) of services had made attempts to reach disabled women through publicity, talks or local partnership working with disability organisations, with lack of resources being cited as the main reason for not doing so. Furthermore, only a quarter offered some form of access to disabled workers, and only three projects had disabled staff in post to respond to disability issues.

Under two-thirds of projects provided disability equality training, which was of varying lengths, and was sometimes part of core training. These training sessions had been delivered from a wide range of sources, sometimes of variable quality, despite attempts by Women's Aid to ensure good practice. Overall, awareness, attitudes and understanding of disability and domestic violence issues (assessed by looking at the knowledge and attitudes displayed in the discursive parts of the survey and at ways in which domestic violence organisations utilised disability equality training, as well as employed, engaged and learned from disabled women) appeared to be low in the majority of domestic violence organisations. In many cases there were no measures in place either to improve attitudes and knowledge or to reach disabled women and involve them in the service. The findings from the surveys indicated a clear need for all domestic violence services to undertake disability equality training provided by respected organisations with expertise in this area, and preferably by disabled women consultants, where possible, as an example of best practice, following the principle 'Nothing about us without us.'

Overall, the study findings revealed that, despite the best of intentions, domestic violence services for disabled women nationally were patchy and sometimes minimal. The identified problems in accommodating and/ or providing services for disabled women affected by domestic violence included awkward stairs in properties, problematic old buildings, building regulation constraints, inaccessible rooms, no disability access/adaptations at all in many, and no funding to improve properties, resulting in widespread inability to comply properly with the Disability Discrimination Act, often also due to absence of resources. It should be noted that many domestic violence organisations do not own their own properties, and hence are reliant on other organisations to provide and modify the buildings in which their services operate, but this does not help the disabled woman who needs to access the services.

The lack of detailed disability equality training within many organisations created further barriers to effective services for disabled women, as many projects consequently lacked confidence about addressing disability requirements in terms both of practical issues and of understandings of disabled women's needs. This lack impacted critically on attitudes and on whether disabled women were likely to feel comfortable accessing such services or indeed to be welcomed by them. To improve their responses, domestic violence organisations identified the need for more fully accessible outreach services, refuge accommodation, and other safe housing for disabled women, better publicity and advertising to improve the information available, more awareness of disabled women's needs, and clear and fully developed disability policies. Better partnership working with disability and disabled people's organisations was also highlighted as being needed.

While the majority of specialist domestic violence organisations were able to liaise with disability organisations when required, few had developed partnerships in place. As the discussion below shows, disability organisations were generally not focused on the issue of domestic violence and were therefore unlikely to provide the type of inter-agency partnership that good practice requires. In general, the survey concluded that until a wider and embedded shift regarding disability occurs at management and frontline levels, as well as among frontline workers, domestic violence services for disabled women are likely to remain inadequate and gaps in provision unfilled. Lack of resources and funding were the main difficulties identified in the study and the current uncertain funding climate is likely to create further difficulties for domestic violence services in addressing any remaining gaps in their services.

However, on a general level, the lack of engagement with disabled women, through advice and involvement, invites the question of whether this lack of services leads in turn to the under-use of domestic violence services by disabled women, which further compounds the lack of services, and so on in a vicious circle. To build on the good work already conducted in some projects, the importance of issues of disabled women being embedded at both operational and management levels as a core issue in domestic violence services was clearly identified.

Disability and disabled people's organisations

Although domestic violence may not be directly relevant to the work of some disability and disabled people's organisations, most would be expected to have some contact with disabled women experiencing abuse. Consequently, having policies and processes in place for monitoring, basic information provision and referral to domestic violence services could be expected. Tellingly, the survey of disabled people's organisations showed that 53 organisations did not work on domestic violence at all and, while the remaining 73 offered limited responses, they rarely considered domestic violence 'their' issue and reported very few abused disabled women approaching them for support.

Around 5 per cent of disability organisations had domestic violence policies in place and all had been approached for assistance. Where routine enquiry was included in the policy, this was likely to highlight the issue and encourage women to approach the organisation for help and support. Lack of staff and funding capacity were given as the reasons for a lack of development and focus on domestic violence. Some used wider 'vulnerable adults' policies to respond to domestic violence or automatically signposted women to specialist domestic violence services. Disability organisations seldom asked their service users about domestic violence or viewed it as an important issue for women using their services. Over three-quarters had no provision, while around a tenth (12 projects) offered some provision which included, variously, very basic advice and counselling, emergency/crisis care, and outreach, and in some cases housing services, referrals, signposting and a wider hate crimes advocacy service. Just under a third of the survey respondents liaised with other groups (Women's Aid, refuges, domestic violence forums, housing associations, and both children's and adults' social services) regarding disabled women experiencing domestic violence. A tiny minority were members of their local domestic violence forums with the majority not knowing that they existed. Moreover, only seven organisations had offered domestic violence training to staff or volunteers. However, these findings have to be seen in the context of disability organisations being funded to deliver narrow welfare services with extremely limited resources, often making it difficult for them to address domestic violence. Some had no funding at all. The few that were embracing the issue felt that disabled people's organisations needed to develop an improved awareness of domestic violence, to build links with existing domestic violence services, and to have the resources to recruit dedicated staff who could provide specific support to disabled women affected by domestic violence.

While understanding of the complex interplay of disability and domestic abuse was lacking within both sectors, disabled people's and disability organisations tended perforce to prioritise disability as the key identity for their service users over issues of gender and violence. This was reflected in the findings from the national survey which showed that very few disabled women felt it was worth accessing support from disability organisations for help with domestic violence issues. The low level of awareness about domestic violence coupled with the lack of resources meant that questions were not routinely being asked about domestic violence and that responses to any disclosures were also likely to be inadequate, especially given the lack of awareness among staff about how to access and refer to specialist domestic violence services. Indeed, several disability organisations demonstrated limited awareness of gender issues overall, or of violence against women in particular, and some had only male staff, making them less likely to respond adequately to domestic violence.

The general lack of specialist domestic violence service provision – lack of accessible refuges, outreach services and information – was seen by those disability organisations that had developed some good practice as reinforcing the dependency of disabled women on perpetrators of violence. Inadequate care packages were consistently singled out as the factor that led to women entering into and remaining in dependent relationships, exacerbated further if they had dependent children. Training, information, financial resources, better multi-agency work and specialist posts were the principal areas of need identified by disability organisations. In relation to disabled women, the importance of better information about available services, recognition of abuse by PAs and other carers, agreements about the transfer of care packages, and the development of accessible refuges and other services were underlined.

The shortage of resources coupled with a lack of knowledge and awareness in both the disability and domestic violence sectors identified by the national surveys means that disabled women are less likely than non-disabled women to access support and help when they need it, and this is also likely to feed women's fears about institutionalisation if domestic violence is disclosed. Disabled women facing domestic violence are thus less likely to be informed about their options and more likely to be left unprotected. In order to address some of the existing gaps, better partnerships, using formal and informal channels, between the two sectors were considered crucial.

Following on from this discussion of service responses to disabled women experiencing domestic violence within both the domestic violence and disability sectors, the next section discusses women's help-seeking processes and the responses they received from professionals and agencies in their various localities.

Women's help-seeking

Several of the women we interviewed had never sought help, formal or informal, for domestic violence and abuse that they were experiencing. Sometimes women did not recognise their experiences as abuse, as discussed in the previous chapter, especially when it was not physical – 'And I didn't even think of it as abuse. The word. Funny the word didn't even enter my mind, that I was being mentally abused. I didn't know' – which then affected the decisions they made about doing something about their situations. In other cases, women blamed themselves and had not told anybody, because they believed they had no choice:

> But what can I do, where could I go? I'd got three young children. I kept everything quiet because you do blame yourself, you know, 'He's had a bad day at work.'

Even those women who felt strong in other aspects believed they could not reveal what was happening in their private lives and look for help. Women known for their work around disability issues in their locality especially felt they could not disclose the abuse, which in turn served to isolate them further:

> It wasn't that I went to bed hungry certain nights or whatever, it's that complete isolation that there really isn't anyone to turn to. And partly, if you do turn to someone, the shame of it is enormous. And even more because I'm a disability equality trainer... I mean, I went on a course with social services on how to train people around issues of abuse for vulnerable adults...and there I was being abused at the same time. And you're kind of stuck in the situation that...I don't know. I'm just too proud.

Some women who had professionals in their lives already did not look for help because of being made to feel they were to blame for their situations, while their abusive partner-carers were seen as, in the words of one woman, 'absolutely brilliant'. In a case where the health visitor colluded with the abuser, for instance, a woman was left feeling powerless to do anything:

> She came one day and was really aggressive, saying I was killing myself... so she reinforced him but he was stood behind her laughing and smirking. He never left me alone with anybody and if he did it was like, 'I'll be back in half an hour.'

The absence of a relationship of trust and the fear of being judged were mentioned by some women as barriers to disclosing or seeking help. Women who had negative experiences with helping agencies and professionals from earlier in their life did not trust them enough to reveal their abuse experiences, especially where the abuse was mental and emotional:

> They were people to be feared. They were the people who were going to come and look at you and scrutinise you. I was being scrutinised enough. So the trust wasn't there. Agencies hadn't given me any reason to trust them until much later on. But then I'd still say it was very confusing because a lot of mine was mental abuse. And because of my disability it was so subtle. It was actually a doctor that said it to me that way.

Even where professionals did pick up on women's abuse, women required a positive indication that they would be assisted by them, without which they were generally reluctant to disclose, as the following shows:

> But I wasn't picking up that they were picking up. And I wasn't picking up that they was having any sympathy. They never give me any indication that they would support me. None. If they'd have gone out on a limb like that social worker did when I got placed in the bungalow, if they'd have just gone out on a limb. If there was intervention earlier, you know. But then maybe they're still only learning. I don't know. Because disabled people

are…it's not been that long that disabled people have been speaking out for themselves. Twenty years. What's 20 years? It's nothing.

Fear of losing their independence, or in some cases of being judged as a 'bad mother' and losing their children, were the two main reasons for women's fear and reluctance to tell anyone. Consequently, women put up a front to indicate that 'I'm coping okay, I'm fine. I'm fine,' but explained that this had ultimately taken a serious emotional toll. However, for a few women, their sense of pride had acted as a barrier to seeking help:

> Mostly, pride really…I lived this lovely independent life in the community. I fund my own care package. It's all hunky dory, lovely, lovely. But actually no, there wasn't anyone I could talk to.

Accommodation and physical accessibility also formed significant barriers for women in seeking help. Many of them believed they could not be accommodated according to their needs as support services rarely had fully adapted accommodation. They were sometimes also reluctant to leave their own housing if it had been adapted to their requirements. Accessibility was of great importance to disabled women interviewees and they talked about this in terms of both physical access and accessibility in a broader sense of attitudes and sensitivity.

Not having information about existing services and believing there was nowhere to go were further frequent barriers to women's help-seeking, especially for those women who were unable to make a phone call themselves or to leave their homes, and the absence of realistic alternative accommodation was a major factor for almost all the women interviewed:

> And I did think about phoning like phone lines and things like that. But it was quite difficult physically to pick up the phone and find the number and dial it. But also it felt kind of a bit futile really because you know it had to be a big thing to make [partner's name] go away, really. I couldn't ever go to a safe house…I know it's not really a real option for a lot of people. But you know I had to use a hoist. I have an electric bed. I have lots of support needs.

Interviewees commonly believed that refuges and related domestic violence services were not 'for them', which further served to form a barrier to seeking assistance. Some women did not feel they could ring agencies for help as they felt different and perceived that services would be unable to offer them the support they needed as disabled women. This was especially difficult, as shown below, for women who had to go to great lengths to seek out information:

...for various reasons I think a lot of disabled women are not so aware of the resources that are there to support you. I mean, I didn't know what was out there for people like me. I didn't associate it with me. I thought, 'That's not me.'

For example for Deaf women you don't overhear things in passing. You don't hear general conversation, you don't hear stuff on the radio, for example. You don't just pick things up like hearing people do. You have to hone in on things, make an effort, deliberately seek information out. You have to make a point of it. There's this thing about information not getting to you or you not realising that the things are meant for you.

Additionally, not being understood by white professionals and agencies and racism were real fears and/or actual experiences for some BMER disabled women, who believed they had few options other than to tolerate their situations. This left BMER women extremely isolated and unsupported:

When I have opened up about something, I haven't been understood. They just didn't know where I was coming from. If anything, I felt like they were being very disrespectful, not hearing me... I've had that experience and I don't want that again. The help that I need isn't out there. That's the reality...locality, ignorance, racism. I'm not afraid to say that anymore. I'm being judged by the colour of my skin before anything...I've experienced this in the so-called disability organisation where I was judged for my colour.

BMER women living in predominantly white areas, in particular, thought services could not support them as both disabled and black women – 'It's just a no win situation for me.' In these situations, and especially where some groups of BMER women (such as some African-Caribbean women) had had negative experiences with statutory services, they believed they had to rely on themselves: 'The only choice I've had is to find my own way, really...it's really me helping me out, really.' Given their limited options, women with no recourse to public funds, owing to having lived for a limited length of time in this country, had stayed in the abusive situation until reaching a point of extreme crisis, at which time they had contacted the police.

Not being taken seriously or not being believed by agencies and professionals were also barriers to reporting for the lesbian women in our study:

I don't ever think that they would fundamentally take it really, really seriously. I don't know if that's my scepticism about the police or whether that's true. But I think that people still have this vision of abusers to be male, to be stronger.

She was stronger than me but she was really skinny. And in those kinds of situations there are no bruises left to be seen. It was her word against mine.

Who they told and the help they were given

Although several women in the study had not sought any form of help, of those who had, more women were likely to have used informal networks of support, including friends, siblings, neighbours and parents. They were equally divided as to whether these contacts had been helpful or unhelpful.

Telling their mothers (or their mothers seeing what was happening) was the only disclosure that took place for some women:

Eventually, I started telling her everything. Me mum could see, and to the point where she started coming round like once a week and, really that once a week was…she'd come round and cook dinner and sort me out…but really she was keeping an eye on things and making sure I was alright before she left at night.

Telling their parents had been an extremely difficult thing to do for other women but once this happened, it enabled them to leave abusive partners – 'I just sat there all night with them and didn't say anything and then the next day I said "I'm scared of him."' In a few cases, staying with their parents had provided an important stop-gap before being re-housed, especially for women who did not require adapted accommodation. Younger women had found parents helpful and supportive but, in a few cases, controlling and dominating. When a woman returned home after domestic violence, this might give her parents an opportunity to be in control of her life again, especially if she had had to make painstaking efforts to break away in the first place. Such cases reveal the contradictions for disabled women between care and control by significant others in their lives.

For some interviewees whose siblings had worked out what was happening, their intervention had been experienced positively – for example, giving the woman a leaflet with contact numbers, information about abuse, and putting her in touch with support services. However, in some situations, a woman's reluctance to name the abuse left family members powerless to do anything until after separation. Some women had limited contact with their family, who felt uncomfortable with the fact that they were disabled, while some had no family at all to turn to for help. For those who were well connected and networked, peer support was significant and something they relied on heavily in sharing experiences and information.

Aside from support from their family and friends, many women had not sought any kind of assistance, even after separation. This was especially so for BMER women who had experienced quite profound isolation, which had lessened for those who were either able to access specific services or had some mobility. Contacting the researchers to give an interview was the first time that some women had spoken about their experiences to an outsider. This was often a part of the process of them recognising that they had to, or wanted to, deal with some of the painful memories around what had happened and it was their way of initiating this process. A couple of women were using writing as a way of dealing with their experiences of domestic violence and sharing their stories.

Believing abuse to be physical and having grown up in a situation where their fathers were violent towards their mothers, some women in the study had only started the process of naming the abuse after separation from their abusive partner-carers. One woman had recently started to study domestic violence and saw it as 'part of the healing that I need to go through':

> It just didn't click to me that psychological abuse and bullying and all that is abuse. So it was only after he'd gone, really, and I started to have time for myself and that I realised, 'Oh my god I have been abused, he was abusing me.' And my friends were saying they'd noticed…they noticed that. It was only then, afterwards, I noticed that I was being abused. And, obviously, with me studying and everything now, I'm more aware of what's going on and that's when I thought, 'Yes, let me contribute something towards this' and also it's part of…it's part of me acknowledging that as well.

Recognising that they needed help to deal with the emotional impacts of their experiences, a number of the women had made attempts to seek help some time after the abuse had ended (in some cases years later) but had encountered mixed responses. For a woman who had spent a year looking for sensitive support, there was the gradual realisation that there was nothing available:

> I've started to look for some kind of therapy but, to be honest, I can't find a counsellor that understands disability equality because a lot of them, I find, are a bit…they still see me as a dependent person, not who I am. You know, the stereotype of a disabled woman who can't do anything for herself, kind of thing. And that's really knocked me. And I can't get into a therapeutic relationship with someone that doesn't understand that. I find that really hard. The fact that I'm gay gives it another angle. The fact that most counselling services aren't physically accessible. It's been quite hard to find… I haven't found anyone yet. And, in a way, I'd quite like to talk about it now. I haven't talked about it properly before… I've looked

a bit nationally as well. And a friend's been looking for me as well and he's quite horrified that there, actually, really isn't very much out there…

Women had often spent years trying to deal with the effects of abuse and only a few had found supportive groups that were assisting them to come to terms with what had happened. Lifting the blame from themselves, recognising they had done the best for their children given the circumstances, learning not to be overwhelmed by their feelings of guilt, and respecting themselves, were among the things that women valued about positive support:

Because, even 40 years later…and this is how I explained it to the tutor. Everything was there, all jumbled up, but, with that course, everything slotted into place and it's helping me begin to feel like a whole person again. And that blame is removed from me… It's not just what you suffer, it's what you put yourself through when you've left. The guilt, knowing you've affected your children. Me not actually knowing until six months ago how my children were affected.

Living in smaller neighbourhoods where they were known to local residents offered women some protection against abusive partner-carers, as the existence of such support offered to a woman sometimes isolated the abuser. At times, neighbours were found to be more helpful than statutory services:

And my next door neighbour…this is nothing to do with council or social, this is all people around me that are more use than them. I would have preferred social being more use, but definitely more use round here. My next-door neighbour gave me more help and she got to my brother and my brother came up.

Everyone, I mean everyone round here… I mean, I've lived here all my life, apart from two years when I lived in […] with […]. Apart from that, I've lived here all my life. So I know a lot of people. I can go down the street and speak to people, or nod to people or whatever. It's just…it's my village.

Remaining in their own accessible accommodation within their own local networks was of great importance to some women, which then helped them to deal with the abusive situation:

Because it's my house, it's been adapted for me and everything, and it's my village. It's where I've been brought up and…I know a lot of people round here, friends or just people I just see every now and again. And it's just easy. I mean, I know it's adapted for me round here in the house itself, but the village too…you just go down and it takes you a couple of minutes and you're down to the supermarket.

Responses from formal agencies

Findings from our national study show that the police, social services/adult services, and housing were the top three agencies women had contact with. This was followed by refuges/domestic violence services and disability organisations. In some cases, this contact with agencies was not at the time of the abuse but occurred later on. When asked if their needs had been met, women almost always said no, although there were a few positive examples given of when their needs were met. This included two refuges (where they had adapted accommodation), three domestic violence services, one disability organisation, one mental health support service, one social worker, and two police officers. However, when asked which agency had been most and least helpful, 80 per cent of women mentioned adult social services as least helpful, followed by the police in 50 per cent of cases, along with GPs and solicitors. Those agencies mentioned as most helpful included domestic violence services in 17 per cent of cases and disability organisations in 10 per cent of cases. The rest of the interviewees had not been able to identify any agencies at all as 'most helpful'.

Although a range of professionals in the study encountered disabled women through their work, none, except for one sole worker, had picked up on the domestic violence that women were living with. Thus, carers, social workers and other professionals going to women's homes had failed to pick up on the abuse, and became aware of it only if women disclosed it themselves. Professionals frequently focused only on the impairment and on women's ability to deal with what was happening in relation to it, especially in cases where the impairment had developed later in life. A number of women reported suffering from depression, which again had been addressed by the social worker without any questions being asked about what was happening in the home. It was often automatically assumed that such depression was caused by being disabled, a throwback perhaps to the pre-social model focus on 'adjustment' rather than independence and empowerment.

Some women, who had the courage to disclose a little, hoped that professionals would either ask more or take some action, something that rarely appeared to happen. Even where the issue could easily have been pursued, professionals were often reported not to have followed things up. Not being asked by professionals, coupled with reluctance to disclose, maintained the secrecy of abuse for many disabled women.

Where abuse had been disclosed, in a few cases there had been one professional in a long line of encounters who provided a lifeline for women, sometimes through referring to an agency for support or assisting with re-housing issues. Where professionals knew about the dynamics of domestic violence and had made a positive response to women, this made a crucial difference to the way that some women were able to respond to their situations. In such cases, women were often surprised that notice of the situation had been taken by the professional and a supportive response provided:

> He was different, and he noticed what was going on because he'd worked a number of years with vulnerable disabled adults and I'm sure he came across somebody like me before, because he just knew. I could tell he knew. The way he was looking at me. I could tell he knew. He did the best thing he could have done. He introduced me to the [disability organisation]. He put it across to my ex-husband that it would do me good, maybe, to meet up with other disabled people like myself. He was very clever.

Police responses

> I did phone the police once and they were OK when they came but, by then, he had left in his car and I told them I would be OK. I felt that they felt sorry for me, like what's that word, patro...what is it, patronised, because I was pathetic and couldn't talk well and they had to struggle to understand me...

> R: Yes the police were concerned about my safety but he'd gone by then and they said to call straight back if he turned up again and wanted to know about whether I had safe places to go to and everything. They were OK. They asked if they could get in touch with anyone for me.

> I: Did they mention domestic violence officers or units to you? Lots of police stations have that sort of special unit these days.

> R: No, they didn't. I don't know anything about that and I wish I had. They might have helped more.

> The police, a couple of times. Once when he broke the crutches, and once when he threw the coffee. On the first occasion, he was fined and put on probation. Second time, I dropped the charges. I didn't want to pursue it, like I said before. The police were OK till then, but then they looked at me as if I was stupid. It wasn't the domestic violence officers, just the ordinary police I think. They did try to pick him up after the incident. They issued a warrant for him.

> He hits me, he abuses me, he gets away with it. He needs to be taught a lesson. I pay with my pain, but it's worth it. Police doesn't help me, not council, not solicitor...all bureaucracy and excuses. I'm thinking of chaining myself to No. 10 Downing Street as I have no other options.

Although responses varied, disabled women reported more unhelpful responses from the police than positive ones. Some of the experiences interviewees had had with the police demonstrated a substantial lack of insight into the nature of their abuse experiences. In a few cases, the police told women to 'leave him until the morning' or 'let him sleep it off' and, at times, warned women they would have their children taken away from them or placed on the child protection register if they continued to live in the situation. Contrary to women's expectations, police officers provided few, if any, offers of support to them:

> I didn't know where to go, who to talk to. And I believed that the police would somehow solve it for me and [they] didn't. And their response was, 'Well, if you take him back it's your problem again.' And it was, like, you have no idea why I'm taking him back. I'm taking him back because it's that or he'll boot my door anyway. And so you convince yourself that you'll try and make it work because you sort of have to.

Where partners were also carers, it was sometimes assumed by police officers that arrests could not be made, illustrating the contradiction for disabled abused women who are often dependent on their abusers for care and thus have limited options in such situations, as the following quote shows:

> R: And ironically, as well, one night she smashed a window at the front door, actually, and someone in the street must have called the police. The police came round and she was very drunk and the policeman came in and said, 'Oh is everything alright?' And I was like, 'Oh yeah, it's fine.' And he said, 'Oh, we could arrest her for breaking the window but we won't because she's got to look after you.' And you're kind of like, 'Oh, OK then.' And I didn't even want to say, you know, well actually...
>
> I: And if they had arrested her?
>
> R: And if they'd taken her away then I wouldn't have got to bed that night. I wouldn't have got to the toilet. You're really, really stuck.

In complete contrast, we were informed of situations where a support organisation had alerted the police to a potential threat to a disabled woman's life, and they had responded very positively, illustrating the importance of institutional advocacy. Women interviewees were particularly positive about the police response where police officers were proactive and offered helpful options. Indeed, women emphasised that a more proactive response from the police was essential for disabled women, as many are in particularly vulnerable situations, living in extreme fear of their abusers, and are scared to disclose:

> They could give lots of advice about, you know, go here or go there or come to interview me on my own when he wasn't there to find out a bit more about my situation generally. I mean, I do remember ringing up and

telling them, 'Well, he's just been here' and they would come and look and 'Oh, we can't find him.' I go 'But he will come back tonight.' 'Well, ring us again.'

One woman who had moved on from her abuse experiences was motivated to raise awareness amongst the police and had contacted the local police to share with them the barriers that had existed for her around help-seeking:

I said to her [police officer], basically, what would you have done if I'd have come to you? I didn't phone anyone up because he'd always smashed the phone up to stop me from ringing someone. So I didn't phone anyone up. But, if I had actually got to a phone, what would you have done if I'd have got in touch with you?… Someone in the domestic violence unit at [the] police station, they got in touch with me and basically he said, 'Can I come out and see you?' So he came out and he said, 'If we'd come to you and you were distressed and all the rest of it, not showing any signs – nothing, no slap marks or whatever – we still would have taken him away.'

Only a minority of the women had taken out injunctions against their partners, often going to see solicitors themselves. Those who had taken no civil protection had been afraid of the consequences of doing so, fearing that their abusers would become worse in their perpetration of abuse as a result of this.

Adult services and social care

Social services have still not improved – not sensitive to the needs of disabled women. They have a very naïve attitude, like that your family will be supportive if you are disabled.

And I was active, going out, etc., getting around and able to speak for myself a bit – imagine how much worse it could have been… In theory they are sensitive, in practice they weren't – they go for the cheaper option. That is why I got the cheapest option or nothing.

As already noted, most women could not identify a single statutory agency that had been helpful. Despite the fact that many disabled women had regular contact with social care professionals, disturbingly, our interviewees' experiences of social care/adult services were almost entirely negative:

Social services, yeah they came, they said, 'Do you need an ambulance?' and then they said all they could offer was […] House. There were no refuges available for a disabled woman, they said. That place was a Cheshire Home! I wasn't going there…totally inappropriate and I'd just get dumped there. All they offered was an institution! There was no accessible space at the refuge. So they said, 'Well, if you won't take that, there is nothing we can do for you. Sorry. Goodbye,' and just left me in the situation! Can you believe that? They said that was all they could do, so tough really. And they left me!

This lack of insight was reinforced by the experiences of another woman who reported:

For example they [social services] could only think to send me to a completely inappropriate disabled care home. It was outrageous. I couldn't even consider going there. They also know nothing about domestic violence, not really. Not for disabled women, anyway. Maybe for others they do, but not disabled.

In general, social workers in the study were failing to respond positively to women's situations and, in particular, were failing to understand the nature of abuse against disabled women:

I did actually have a social worker then and, when she came round, she knew…we went out for a walk at our village and she knew what had been happening and she knew just a little bit, the shouting was still going on. And I told her that I was having a lot of hassle and, well, she didn't understand because she didn't really know what to do. I honestly don't know whether she said 'me phone her' but, I mean, that would be difficult, as well, because of him being here all the time. And I couldn't really phone people out. I didn't have a mobile phone because he didn't agree with mobile phones…she was no good, she never came back to see what was happening. She never kept up with it so there was no aftercare or anything like that…but, at the time, I suppose I really, really did want someone to come and help me.

Social workers who were aware of domestic violence and had been proactive had become a lifeline for a few women. Simply telling a woman they knew what was going on and doing their best to help her to remove herself from the situation through exploring the options, or putting her in contact with a disability or domestic violence organisation, made a huge difference. 'How would I have ever reached out to anybody if that social worker hadn't have gone out on a limb for me?' was a question posed by one of the women we interviewed.

Some BMER women did not trust social workers after having had negative experiences. Some also reported problems with care workers who were unwilling to carry out certain care tasks for a black woman and this issue then being badly dealt with by the social care agency: 'Because I kept on voicing about the cultural needs, I ended up not getting any care for over a year.' Where this happened, women might be left to receive care from their family members only, creating greater dependence on informal care. Thus, it was claimed that neglect for black women not only came from individuals known to a woman but also from those in organisations.

In a small number of cases, children and families social services had placed children in foster care when women and children left known abusers because no other support could be provided. This had led to the women concerned spending considerable time and emotional energy trying to get their children back. Generally, for those women who had left their homes due to domestic violence, adult services were thought to lack understanding of their support needs and were seen to be inflexible in terms of the support and care that was put in place. In the main, women painted a fairly damning picture.

Disability organisations

Few of the women we interviewed had accessed disability or disabled people's organisations, and where they had it was mainly for general advice and they had not disclosed domestic violence and abuse. The reasons for this varied – some women did not feel comfortable disclosing abuse and others said there were no appropriate settings to do this. Among BMER women a perception existed that disability organisations were white and ill-informed about their issues, something that was reinforced by negative responses when some women had approached their local disability groups. Overall, the majority of women had been unaware of disability organisations.

In those few cases where women had been in direct contact or where professionals had introduced them to a supportive disability or disabled people's organisation, being in a supportive environment enabled these women to become stronger and finally leave the abusive situation at a time when the abuse had been escalating, as in the following quotes:

> The disability people's movement has been so empowering for me, hugely empowering…

> The course was just a ten week course so he felt, 'Oh, that'll be it and she's only going talking to other disabled people, she'll be fine.' What he didn't know was I was being empowered by a strong disabled people's movement. And, when I went for that course, I mean, god, I can talk now, I can talk a glass eye to sleep. But [then] I didn't speak. I spoke if I was spoken to. I was very quiet. And, when I went on that course, that's how I was. And I said 'Sorry' every five minutes. And they knew, because obviously they'd experienced things. That's the reason why they were doing the course in the first place. It was one of the trainers who knew

because she'd said my life mirrored hers. And, by the end of that course, I got an award for staying in a 'sorry-free zone'. But it was a start, you know. And then they were trying to get disability equality trainers, they saw a potential, but they also saw that I was suffering systematic abuse. So then they encouraged me. And, to cut a long story short, from doing index cards I became Chairperson eventually of the organisation. And it took me two years to leave him. But really it wasn't just that…the violence was escalating because he noticed the confidence in me. He noticed I was changing.

Having lived with abuse for a long time, even where women had positive responses from disability organisations, it took them some time to begin sharing their abuse experiences. Being asked about it by someone they had learnt to trust helped them to start opening up and such positive input has continued to have ramifications for the rest of their lives:

They were one of the leading ones to teach about the medical model and the social model of disability. I'm still involved down here because I knew what power that organisation had and what it gave me. What power it gave me. But, if all other organisations would learn from organisations like that! They really get things done.

In the case of one woman, the disabled people's organisation was continuing to provide support and activities after a year. In some cases, however, women had found disability organisations had lacked understanding of their situations, had offered no support, and had made it quite clear they were not interested.

I didn't try them, they don't know anything about it. 'Not their business' is what they think, if they think at all.

Often the disabled organisations, they have not taken on domestic violence at all, not part of their remit, they think. They don't see it…just don't see it, do they? It passes them by.

I don't feel that there is very much, if any, awareness among disability-led, Deaf-led organisations of domestic violence. They need to be able to signpost disabled and Deaf women appropriately, to good support services certainly. You don't really see anything about it in those services.

Domestic violence services

Only a minority of the women in our study had accessed domestic violence organisations or refuges and their experiences had varied considerably:

The facilities were excellent. You could tell they'd liaised with disabled people because it was that good.

Oh, god, I went to some awful ones and they were horrendous.

Even when I ended up in a refuge, I was seen as a problem. A burden. And the social services down here would not allow me to have a care worker that could take me out as well as come in. They could come in and make my meals, they could come in and do my washing, but not to take me out. So that burden fell on my son. Again, I felt like a prisoner. I felt like, 'It's your fault, this. You've been here before, you're in your probably sixth refuge.' You know, it just felt like I was old news. Even in the refuge, I felt imprisoned again, like I said. And it's because the pressure they're put under, I realise now. I didn't then, and because there's only limited funds and things like that, they're more willing to help them that'll help themselves. Well, the majority of us don't help ourselves, do we. We need their help.

I didn't approach the disability organisations or the domestic violence organisations, the refuge was not accessible. If I had been able to use these facilities, or if they had access, I would have left much sooner and not suffered so much violence but they weren't.

Refuges? I never thought they were for disabled women.

Overall, more positive responses were highlighted by women for domestic violence services than for disability organisations, but, while some positive work had been undertaken, the main difficulty identified with refuges was their lack of accessibility as many of the women's voices above highlight.

Interviewees who had accessed refuges that had given considerable thought to accessibility issues, and made appropriate provision for disabled women, were extremely positive about the service they had received. In general, with one exception, refuges had been accessed by those women with fewer support needs. A few had not accessed refuge accommodation itself, but had been supported post-separation by domestic violence services through outreach support.

Where women interviewed had negative experiences of accessing refuges, they spoke at length about the sometimes paternalistic attitude and approach of workers to them as disabled women, and generally felt staff were not well equipped to respond to their support needs:

It was like, 'We're going to need to sort this out for her, or we're going to need to sort that out for her.' But it was, like, said in front of me.

It wasn't like, 'What do you think we need to do that would make things easier for you?' Even when I was in [refuge] there was no one to take me shopping… I had to eat and it was left to the other women to take that role on. Well, I think that was really unfair. They're going through their own emotions. Why should that burden be passed to them? And it was exactly the same when I came down here, the other women were asked to look after me. Well, what did that do to my status? I was even lower than what they were. I became even lower down the ladder.

Where women had been given support with their court cases and were accompanied to court by domestic violence workers, this was greatly valued by them:

And the next time I had to go back to court the refuge were fabulous. They arranged for a worker from a refuge in [locality] – there was two of them – to meet me at the railway station and go into court. They couldn't actually go into court, but they were there waiting for me. And they were absolutely brilliant. And they put me on the train again afterwards.

Our interviewees also appreciated the emotional support that was provided by workers, along with the space that was created to share their experiences with other women in the refuge without having to worry about the children:

But, mentally, there was always like [worker] would take the kids off and do fun things with the kids so we could sit and talk about our experiences, because that was important to all of us. So they made time for us as well as, you know, keeping the children entertained.

In a minority of cases, women had continued to receive support through a follow-up service – 'It's something that's for me because I've never had anything for me before' – or had received non-refuge based support. Again, this type of service was something that was highly valued by women.

A few women only had contact with domestic violence services after they had dealt with the abusive situation, but when they were seeking further emotional support to help them deal with the ongoing effects of their past situation, because they were unable to speak in detail to their families:

I felt like I needed to get this out because it's in me now, the experiences and everything, and I can't talk to my mum because they lived through it all before, they're too close. I mean, I've wrote down a lot of this stuff and it's like I still feel I need to share it. And I still hope and I think, 'Well, I don't know, maybe it will help people' and I wonder if it will help someone, and I hope it does.

Sometimes, this contact was very short or limited. However, women's accounts show that disabled women often require support years down the line with what has happened to them from services that are sensitised to their experiences and able to provide appropriate support.

BMER women who were supported by culturally specific domestic violence services spoke very positively about this, mentioning that being able to speak to people who understood their experiences in their own language helped to lessen their isolation and enable them to become more positive about their lives:

> Without them, I would have taken my own life. I have tried to once before. They have helped me with everything, especially emotional support.

> They listen to me and help me a lot. I need to see them regularly to keep my spirits up and make me feel less alone.

The majority of women in our study had little knowledge about domestic violence services. Lack of information about refuges and a perception that refuges were not 'for them', as already noted, were strongly held views:

> I would have liked to have gone to a refuge at one point but I didn't know how to. That was after he'd hit me and I was so upset…but I didn't know what to do. I was living in a flat on my own and I was just so…frightened of him. I was told that refuges were not for people like me, or that's what I thought anyway…but I could have done with that, with getting some support and help and feeling safe. It would have helped so much, but they weren't for women like me.

> I suppose they need to be more accessible – I thought they weren't for me and I couldn't use them. Now I've found out I could have, if I had known, but it didn't feel as though I was the sort of woman who could go there or who they would help or they would want to have there.

> Like I said, they need to deal with domestic violence if women coming to them have had that happen to them. At the moment, they don't think it is their problem. They really don't.

> Refuges? I didn't approach them. I thought they were just for domestic violence and nothing to do with disabled women. I didn't think they were for *me*…

Other agencies

In the absence of knowledge or information about refuges and other domestic violence services, women interviewed sometimes contacted organisations such as the Citizens Advice Bureau, MIND, solicitors or GPs. When they did finally disclose their abusive situations, women taking this route were rarely informed about specialist services for domestic violence, but appreciated this very much when it happened:

And she just said to me, 'You know, you need to talk to somebody. Do you want to tell me what's been going on?' And I told her. And of course I fell apart. She said, 'Look, you're not on your own. I'm going to pop out the room and get this phone number.' And she said, 'It's a direct line. Carry it with you all the time and have you got a phone?' And I said, 'Yes, there's one by the side of the bed.' She said, 'Well, if anything happens like that again, you must ring this number.'

In the main, solicitors were found to be unhelpful, paying little attention to women's safety or to confidentiality. In one case, a solicitor had disclosed a woman's new address to the abuser. Where formal mainstream counselling services had been accessed, these had also been found, often, to be unhelpful:

They obviously didn't pick up how frightened I was and she actually recommended we get back together and that we work at the relationship. But she didn't seem to pick up all the signals or didn't even sort of get me on my own or anything.

Worryingly in another instance, where a woman disclosed abuse to her GP, the doctor told everything to her husband, who was her carer. However, there were a few instances of positive responses, such as where a woman had sought to remove her partner from a jointly owned property and had found the judge to be supportive of her right to live in the property because of the adaptations that had been made. A few women had made use of injunctions in order to prevent their partners from harassing them in a previously shared property. In such cases, women had pursued their cases with the support of family members but, in the main, had not received any formal support.

Advice to other disabled women

When women were asked what advice they would give to other disabled women, the importance of telling someone was repeatedly emphasised:

Try and tell someone who is close by...not keeping it a secret and not to feel ashamed by it. Because that's one of the reasons that they get away with what they do, they play on that. And recognise that it's not acceptable to be abused. And, if you're uncomfortable with something, think it through and try and talk to someone else about it, not necessarily the person that's doing it to you. But see if you can develop strategies to deal with it...because you can minimise things as well. And the law's not up to it. The legal system does not stand up to abuse unless it's really severe and really obvious.

I wonder if they've got any family or friends, if they get in touch with those. Or, if they have a social worker or social services. They need someone

> to lean on. They do need someone to talk to first. Tell someone about it.
> They really need to tell someone about it and talk to someone.

Some women who had remained silent about their abuse for a long time had come to believe that telling someone was critical to disabled women dealing with their situations:

> Talk to somebody. You can go on-line and find an on-line agency or ring somebody up. At the end of the day, they've got to tell somebody.

Being supported to name the abuse was seen as a crucial step for women in dealing with their experiences – 'First they've got to realise that they are in an abusive relationship themselves' – as was the importance of women believing they did not deserve the abuse to which they had been subjected:

> No one ever deserves it...you need to feel you're worth something different. Say to yourself that you are worth more. That is so hard for disabled women, what with all the stuff about women being perfect and beautiful.

Interviewees who had dealt with and survived quite extreme abuse voiced wanting to tell their story to help others in similar situations:

> And I just have been feeling that I really wanted to say 'This happened', to tell other women. So that perhaps my experiences can be of help to other people. I'm not upset about it anymore. When I look back it's like I'm some other woman.

To this end, a few women were engaged in various means of offering help to others, based on what they had learned. This included using writing as a way to deal with their experiences and to share their stories, engaging in drama productions, or working in disability organisations to advocate for attention to be given to issues of domestic violence and disabled women.

Conclusion

The findings of our national study, as discussed in this chapter, show that, despite pockets of good practice, responses to disabled women experiencing domestic violence and abuse are frequently inadequate across the range of sectors, professionals and agencies. Where good practice exists this is usually dependent on the motivation and commitment of individual workers and professionals, and often located within specific domestic violence services and a minority of disability and disabled people's organisations. Not having information about existing services, or believing domestic violence services are not meant for disabled women, along with the lack of real alternatives, act as barriers for women in telling others about their abusive situations and seeking help.

Gaps in services and barriers to effective provision are accompanied by the fact that the needs of abused disabled women are more pronounced due to their isolation and vulnerability to abusers. Thus, substantially *less provision* than that available proportionally to non-disabled women is accompanied by a *greater need* for such focused and specialist services. Disabled women appear, therefore, to lose out *on both counts*. It is crucial in the future that all relevant services, including statutory agencies and both domestic violence and disabled people's sectors, give greater priority to addressing this issue. Up till now, disabled women facing domestic violence and abuse have been ignored and left without assistance from the very agencies that are meant to offer them help and protection.

Notes

1   All service details in the UKROL database are updated biannually; new services and changes to contacts are updated on an ongoing basis. See http://womensaid.org.uk/landing_page.asp?section=0001000100060009.
2   Statistics collected in a day count of women using services.

Chapter 5

Understanding Our History

The Personal is Political

Brenda Ellis and Ruth Bashall

In setting the political and social context for an understanding of disability and domestic violence, the first part of this chapter provides an overview of the struggles by disabled women, since the mid 1980s, to get the violence and abuse we experience onto the national (and international) agenda. The second part of the chapter covers the issues which we think matter in this debate, and are essential in tackling the violence: the abuse of disabled people generally, violence against disabled women and the choices open to disabled women, definitions of disability and the need for a human rights approach to this issue.

This chapter is written from our personal perspectives as two disabled women who have campaigned for many years on violence against disabled women and girls. We are in solidarity with disabled women everywhere who are working to get violence against disabled women on the agenda. We hope that a snapshot of the history of this struggle will help the reader to understand the issues, and the barriers, faced by disabled women who experience domestic violence. It has been, and continues to be, a long struggle, and it is sometimes difficult to put across a sense of positive progress. We ourselves are still in a minority of very few disabled women working on violence against women or indeed on violence against disabled people generally. Sometimes disabled women work with non-disabled allies; sometimes we are in conflict with people whose approach is based on a more protectionist approach that sees us as 'vulnerable adults'. And while some domestic violence and other women's organisations do include disabled women, there is very little in the way of coordinated strategy at either national or local levels. This chapter is written at a time when funds for domestic violence support and prevention work are being severely restricted, as a result of the coalition government's spending cuts. While this may make it, in the short term, more difficult to persuade providers and policy-makers to change, it is more than ever essential that these services and strategies are inclusive of disabled women.

In spite of this challenging context, our discussions while writing this chapter have made us realise that things have moved on, albeit very slowly – in part due to changes in equality legislation, in part because disabled women are more 'out there' at work, in education, in public roles and in the wider society, and are therefore less easy to ignore.

The social model of disability: explaining our lives

The social model of disability is a means of understanding our situation as disabled people; it is also a tool for change. Developed by disabled people in the mid 1970s, the social model challenges the idea that our impairment is *the* problem and that our difference makes us less valid as human beings. It has been a tool for liberation for many disabled people, ourselves included. Few have put this better than Liz Crow, a disabled artist and activist:

> My life has two phases: before the social model and after it. Discovering this way of thinking about my experiences was the proverbial raft in stormy seas. It gave me an understanding of my life, shared with thousands, even millions of other people around the world. (Crow 1996)

Historically, disabled people have been viewed, in many societies, either as social pariahs or as objects of fear and contempt, or more recently as deserving pity. The medical model focuses on the disabled body or mind as the problem. It is disabled people's personal failing that they cannot use inaccessible public transport, or understand complex language, or read small print. Under this model, disabled people, and in particular those that are 'severely disabled' (a term we would not use ourselves!) and have, for example, learning difficulties, severe mental health issues or are non-verbal, are quasi-children, with no adult desires or wishes, and cannot make decisions for themselves. Solutions[1] (particularly in the richer countries) to the 'problem' of disabled people have focused around medical solutions, institutional 'care', segregated schooling and a 'special needs' approach which sets disabled people apart. This approach leaves disabled people with a legacy of low self-esteem, internalised oppression and disempowerment, and, in many cases, as survivors of sexual and physical abuse. The medical model approach has been successfully challenged by disabled people in many areas, but it still informs much policy and practice, including around social care and violence against disabled people: disabled women and men are 'vulnerable adults' who as victims of violence or abuse must be the subject of protection by professionals who have their best interests at heart. These issues are explored further in this chapter.

The social model offers an alternative, and argues that society needs to change in order to include disabled people, by removing the barriers to our inclusion. Society can become inclusive by ensuring that information, communication, environments, education and processes are changed so they are inclusive of everyone, and can, for example, support people who communicate differently to speak out and have their say. Rachel Hurst, a disabled woman and long-term leading light of the UK and international disabled people's movement, sees the social model as central to social change:

> The social model…is the analysis of the situation of a disabled person, defining disability as *the relationship between a person with impairment and the environment, including attitudes, beliefs, climate, architecture, system and services.* (Hurst 2005, p.65)

Hurst also emphasises that:

> The social model analysis is the essential political tool of the disability rights movement, it allows activists to clarify exactly what changes and actions are necessary, to ensure that disabled people's dignity, rights and freedom are guaranteed. It is important to note the difference between the social model as an analytical tool and the actions…needed for social change inherent in human rights. The two, properly understood and applied together, underpin the validation of disabled people as an important and discrete group of human beings. (Hurst 2005, p.65)

This focus on the social model as a tool for change, and on human rights as both the framework and the goal, is key to our approach to violence against disabled women and girls. This is explored in the second half of this chapter.

The social model also sets the context to how we define who is a disabled woman. For us, defining disability is not about using definitions based on seemingly objective but in fact highly suspect medical tests of impairment that are designed for social institutions to set eligibility criteria for one service or another. As disabled women we are burdened with labels and systems which separate us into impairment categories: physical impairment, visual impairment, Deaf women, women with mental health issues, women with learning difficulties. These labels affect how we are seen, how we access services, where the funding comes from, who makes decisions about us. It affects our life chances and our human rights.

To us, disability is about social oppression – so a disabled person is someone with an impairment who experiences exclusion and discrimination.

The issue of who is or is not a disabled person becomes, therefore, a question of context and to a large extent about self-definition. Though the research on which this book is based only included women with physical and sensory impairments, in this chapter and the next, when we talk about disabled women and girls, we are using a social model approach. We are referring to women with physical and sensory impairments, long-term health conditions, learning difficulties or mental health issues who are *disabled by the barriers they face in society*. These barriers may be attitudinal, environmental, legal or institutional, including a lack of basic human rights and choices. In this context, disability is not fixed or inevitable; discrimination can be challenged and solutions found, and impairment does not have to lead to exclusion and oppression. The social model is about change and inclusion, not 'special needs' approaches.

'The personal is political': our histories

When we were asked to contribute to the book, we were asked to talk about our personal histories and why we became involved in work on violence against disabled women and girls. While at first we were reluctant, we realised that our personal experiences since the mid 1980s have been intertwined with political movements that have been key to changing the way that society, in the UK and worldwide, tackles violence against women and girls. So this is our story.

We are both different and yet have much in common: we both came to the UK as young women, we have a long history as feminists and community activists, were mothers and lesbians long before we came to identify as disabled women. We have both been active in the disabled people's movement since the early 1990s. But because ours are individual voices, we have decided to write the first part of this chapter separately, though each of our contributions is the result of much lively discussion. The second part is written together.

Brenda Ellis

I am a disabled activist, feminist and a lesbian. I think it may be useful to describe some of the discrimination I received as a means of trying to explain exactly how disabled women experience this. When I became disabled later in life (in my 40s) I encountered much discrimination and exclusion. I eventually ended up working for 12 years for a pan-London disabled people's organisation, Greater London Action on Disability (GLAD), which campaigned to change many things for disabled people in London and elsewhere – things like legislation, transport, access, inclusion and promoting the social model of disability. I was also a member of the UK Disability Forum Women's Committee.

The connection between feminism and disability at that time was that disability was an optional add-on. Disability was always the poor relation of 'equalities' and it was astonishing just how long it took for disability to be put on the agenda. Disability was seen as a social welfare not a rights issue, and the voices of disabled people were only just beginning to be heard.

I began my disabled life as Women's Officer working for GLAD, after working in a women's centre and in a community centre. Having just become disabled and feeling very negative about myself, I had to deal with a very painful impairment and using a wheelchair for the first time. Never previously having experienced any real illness, it was a shock to come to terms with this new life. I had already experienced what was in store for me when my partner at the time told me she no longer wished to continue the relationship, as she did not envisage a future with a disabled woman! Is this what disabled people had to cope with? I began to find out that it was. I had already experienced difficulties and discrimination at my previous workplace, where we had heavy metal shutters to close on leaving the centre, which with my new impairment I found impossible to do. My work colleagues found it hard to accept that my ability to do certain things had changed. But this was prior to any legislation protecting disabled people, so you had to convince people that you were not 'putting it on', that being unable to do certain things was genuine. I had never been in this position before.

Beginning work at GLAD really was a revelation in many ways. Working with other disabled people was a huge discovery. I had obviously worked with disabled people, mainly women, but had not really understood the issues before. I was well versed in issues of race, gender and sexuality but disability was just not there. I soon learnt about the social model of disability. The early 1990s was a momentous and exciting time for disabled people. There was a lot of activism, where disabled people had come together as never before: we had our own organisations, run by disabled people, we had Rights Now, an alliance of organisations which brought many groups and individuals together to campaign for disability rights legislation. We had direct action by disabled people, stopping traffic and campaigning outside Parliament for 'Rights Not Charity'. GLAD was a huge mover and shaker, in London, in the UK and in Europe. It brought disabled people together to discuss their issues, it campaigned with public bodies and the government for change and inclusion of disabled people and achieved much of the access now taken for granted in London. The social model of disability, though, was the spark for so many of us.

The social model has brought to many disabled people's lives a way they can understand their own oppression and, in sharp contrast to the medical model, it does change lives for the better. I do think this is because the medical model has been so integral to society's way of thinking it is hard to shake it from your mind and open up to a new way to see disability.

The medical model, as we explained at the start of this chapter, looks at disabled people purely in a negative way. The devastating effects of this on generations of disabled people are not to be underestimated. You are also seen as a 'vulnerable' person, a victim. As far as society goes, disabled people have been and are still locked away with no voice, no representation. We are excluded from mainstream society because we are born with or acquire an impairment.

It begins from the day disabled people are born. Are disabled babies welcomed and celebrated as they enter the world? It is still considered a tragedy, a disaster for the family, something most people are afraid of. The medical profession, too, see it as a tragedy and that they must make medical interventions to try to correct the impairment and try to make the child as 'normal' as possible. Disabled children can be put through huge medical trauma having many operations trying to correct a condition that may not be readily improved or change things for that child. Too many disabled children still end up in segregated education, attending impairment-specific schools, for example schools for Deaf people or schools for blind people. In the past, disabled people really were treated as a race apart from mainstream society, and were considered to be 'handicapped, crippled, Deaf and dumb, mongols, blind as a bat, nutters, thick'. Though this language is now generally considered shocking, disabled children and adults still face name calling in the street and on public transport. After I recently moved to a small West Country town, a neighbour called in to introduce herself and said: 'Oh, so you're the crippled lady who has moved in.' Disabled people are still 'other'.

Disabled people have been portrayed negatively throughout history in folklore, culture, religion and history. This has shaped the way society views us. From villains in history, to the 'wicked witch', to the evil characters in James Bond films – all disabled people. No doubt younger people could supply more recent examples than I can! Over generations this has reinforced the stereotypes, discrimination and exclusion of disabled people from mainstream society. This is so ingrained in society that people do not know they are even doing it. We are somebody else's problem. We are always seen in the context of welfare, being cared for and charity. We need to be seen in the context of equal rights, opportunities and citizenship.

In contrast, the social model of disability has given disabled people a way to understand and change our position in society. Disability is NOT your medical impairment or condition, but the inability to take part in society equally to everyone else. It is because society was and is not geared for disabled people to take part in it. The built environment is inaccessible; transport, housing, means of communication, people's attitudes need to change. Disabled people have a slogan: 'Nothing about us without us.' This means we must be involved in having a say in our own lives, we do not need others to make decisions for us, but treat us as equals. Disabled people's lives in the twenty-first century carry the legacy of a vast, complex, historical and social context. This is all relevant to domestic violence and I will try to show how that is.

I joined GLAD after it had held the first ever disabled women's conference in 1992. There were so many disabled women wishing to come to the event that the venue that had been booked was too small; several new venues had to be booked to accommodate all of the women. I think this event was the catalyst for disabled women getting involved and putting forward their issues for the first time. Domestic violence and abuse was one of them.

In my previous job in a women's centre, I had noted that women's domestic violence services were not accessible: refuges were not accessible, and helplines had no minicom or fax for women who needed this form of communication access. Disabled women were not on the agenda. I also dealt with same-sex domestic violence. So when I went to work for GLAD, where part of my work was to set up events and conferences to bring together disabled women, I also had a chance to start campaigning for the inclusion of disabled women into wider society and to try to highlight that many services for women, including domestic violence services, excluded disabled women.

I knew disabled women were suffering in silence and I had heard many anecdotal stories about this from other disabled activists. One story which particularly affected me was of a disabled woman who had two sons who cared for her. Her husband, the abuser, was also her carer. As a mother of two boys aged over 12 she could not take the boys with her to a refuge. As a disabled woman, she could not find a refuge place as there was nowhere accessible and she could not get the personal assistance she needed in the refuge. She ended up going into a residential home, leaving the two sons with the abusive husband still living in her home. I also personally knew of another case where a young woman with learning difficulties had a male partner who was a wheelchair user. He died suddenly and we were all saying to her how sorry we were that her partner had died – she then told us that he had been abusing her for years, controlling her life and taking her disability benefits and that his death had come as a relief to her. Her own mother had told her prior to his death that she would be better off staying with him, as she would not find anyone else who would be interested in her. Even her family colluded in the abuse. She felt she had no one to turn to. Most people took the view that he was doing her a favour by being with her. A stark lesson in how not to make assumptions.

I attended as many meetings as I could in the capital on domestic violence. One involved the great and the good who worked on domestic violence. I asked a very senior woman from a domestic violence organisation what was being done to include disabled women – helplines do not have a minicom, most refuges are inaccessible. The response? 'They are too expensive.' I was absolutely taken aback at this statement. This made me even more determined to stop this discriminatory view and try to get disabled women on the agenda. Disabled women were totally marginalised and excluded.

By the time I left GLAD, domestic violence against disabled women was beginning to be talked about within domestic violence networks, in London at least. I had some successes in getting disability included in the Greater London Domestic Violence Strategy, and my work and that of other disabled women[2] and our allies helped to sow the seed for further work – some refuges improved their access, polices began to change – but we still had a long way to go before an inclusive approach would be adopted. This work continues.

Ruth Bashall

My involvement around violence against women and girls has been both personal and political – in the 1970s as a local feminist activist in East London and in the 1980s as part of my involvement in the Lesbian Mothers Network. I supported a good friend who had been beaten and raped by her former husband when she left to live with a woman, and was part of a frantic search across England, Scotland and Ireland for her children when her ex-husband kidnapped them. A treasured colleague was murdered by her husband, for which he got three years on the grounds of provocation – she was more successful in her life than he was. A young woman was murdered by her husband in my local police station's 'reconciliation suite'. I provided space in my spare room for survivors and their children. And as a volunteer on London Lesbian Line, I listened to and advised many women fleeing abusive relationships. Just around the time that my impairment was becoming an issue, I left a relationship with a girlfriend who I realised I was afraid of. I remember leaving her house after a row in the middle of the night, painfully making my way down the steep stairs from her first floor flat, thinking: 'I couldn't get out of here quickly if things got really out of hand.' And in my early days as a disability rights activist, while campaigning for accessible transport, I met a disabled woman who refused to leave a violent relationship with a disabled man because in her words: 'At least I know it's only him, if I got back to the "home", it'll be three of them and they will rape me.' I felt powerless to do anything but listen.

I was not disabled as a girl and a young woman, but had the privilege of growing up surrounded by disabled people who lived their lives independently, in spite of considerable barriers: to describe Mary M as a 'woman of restricted growth' would be to impose a term she would have rejected. In the 1960s she lived her life as a wage-earning and proud dwarf, independent and alive, in spite of years of institutional abuse in Catholic orphanages. But I had also seen primary school friends who became disabled as a result of a polio epidemic in the 1950s sent off to segregated secondary schools.

When my own impairment started to impact on my independence – on my ability to use what was then totally inaccessible public transport, and most of all on my personal and work relationships – I veered from despair to rage, a not uncommon experience amongst newly disabled people. But with a push from Mary's memory, I was extraordinarily lucky to be 'taken in hand' by three very different disability rights activists. Kath Gillespie-Sells and Keith Armstrong, and later Kirsten Hearn, made me see that impairment was something I could live with, not by conquering it like some macho mountaineer, but by incorporating it into my life and making changes, and that disability was a social not an individual condition. My focus shifted from a women's movement that was fast rejecting me to the then emerging disability rights movement. LANGUID[3] gave me a network of other disabled lesbian and gay men. I discovered the social model, and with it a vibrant, contradictory, passionate movement for the human rights of disabled people. I brought with me my feminist politics and an understanding of the personal as political, the complexities of layers of discrimination and the possibilities of a world free from violence and human rights abuses. Writers such as Audre Lorde[4] and Laura Hershey[5] helped me understand and celebrate the hardships and the beauty of our lives as disabled women. GLAD's *Boadicea Disabled Women's Newsletter* provided us with a forum for debate. And with my newly acquired knowledge of my rights, I got an electric wheelchair and a concessionary Taxicard. I was off!

I have seen so many disabled women and men make similar journeys from despair to liberation. To me that is also the key to what happens to survivors of violence and oppression. First we believe others when they tell us we are not quite human. Then if we survive, we find a lifeline, someone who tells us it does not have to be like this. This is not a linear journey

– powerlessness and despair will not let go that easily, and some do not make it. But change is possible. To me, that change needs to happen through organisations run by disabled people, working with allies – social action organisations, including the many women's organisations and individuals working against violence against women, and groups like Broken Rainbow who tackle domestic violence in the lesbian and gay communities, or Ashiana and the many black, Asian and other organisations working to tackle violence in their communities. Disabled women cannot do this alone, but we must lead.

After years of working outside the system, in 1990 I went to work as a disability officer for a local council in East London, in the borough where I now live. One of my proudest moments was to be able to use a big chunk of my access budget to provide one accessible bedroom, together with other shared facilities, in the two local Asian Women's refuges, Ashiana and Kiran. Today, I am still working alongside these organisations and they still have some of the very few accessible bed spaces for disabled women in London. In 2003, I joined the newly formed Disability Independent Advisory Group (DIAG), acting as a 'critical friend' advising the Metropolitan Police on disability equality. I co-chaired the group with Anne Novis MBE, an activist who is both an inspiration and an ally, and now mainly works on putting hate crime against disabled people on the national agenda. Alongside Louise Shellard and other DIAG members, we focused most of our energies on working with the Met to change the way they respond to disability hate crime and domestic violence. At the time of writing, not only does the Met have an effective system for recording disability hate crime, and local boroughs have begun to deal with cases effectively, but the Met has identified and is addressing the gaps ('disproportionality' in police jargon) in the way it deals with domestic violence crimes against disabled women. There is more work to be done, but we set the foundations for good practice. Anne Novis and I are part of a hate crime advisory group to the Ministry of Justice, but I have yet to get a foot in the door on domestic violence. It remains to be seen if a change of government and of political priorities, coupled with drastic cuts to so-called non-essential resources, will see this work through.

I am now the chair of an organisation of disabled people, Disability Action Waltham Forest (see www.disabilityactionwf.org.uk/staysafe), which at the time of writing is just one year into a project to support disabled people experiencing hate crime, bullying, and domestic and institutional violence. There are more details of this project in the next chapter.

Fighting violence against disabled women: some history[6]

> All forms of prejudice have at their heart a refusal to identify with a person's reality, setting them apart from common humanity. This is a very important part of the prejudice experienced by disabled people, based as it often is on the assumption that the quality of our lives is too poor that they are not worth living – and therefore an unwillingness to identify with our reality. (Morris 1996, p.6)

There have always been disabled women involved in the struggle for human rights – women like Sojourner Truth and Rosa Luxemburg. But as *disabled* women we have been mostly invisible:

> For women with disabilities to break free from the chains of oppression there must be a recognition that the personal is political and that their experiences are a direct consequence of the social, economic and political structures which place them on the margin of the margin. (Begum 1990, p.77)

Nevertheless, tackling violence against disabled women is grounded in the history of the movements for equality and emancipation of the second half of the twentieth century. The disabled people's movement, like the women's or black rights movements of the 1960s and 1970s, was not the first wave of a movement for emancipation. Disabled people had been challenging institutionalisation, discrimination and our treatment as quasi-children for generations, but in the UK the movement that began with the Union of the Physically Impaired Against Segregation (UPIAS) in 1972 firmly placed 'disability' within a social context, for the first time challenging the prevailing view of impairment (our physical, mental or other 'differences') as *the* problem. It sought to put disability firmly in the context of other movements for social justice and equality. Apart from the social model, one of the movement's primary principles was and is the right to independent living – to make choices about our lives, to have the support to live life in the community, to have relationships and, if we wish, have children on the same basis as anyone else.

Significantly, though this is not always obvious in the literature, disabled women, many of them feminists, were involved in the early groups such as UPIAS and much of the discourse was shaped by a feminist approach to the personal as political, and by more inclusive ways of organising. From early on, disabled feminists began to set up their own groups and challenged both the patriarchal attitudes of the disabled people's movement and the disablism of the women's movement. Like black feminist groups, such as Southall Black Sisters, groups such as Sisters Against Disablement (SAD) sought to change a monocultural approach, for example questioning how to balance a woman's right to choose a late abortion on grounds of impairment with the rights of disabled people. While the failure at that time of most feminist groups to take these concerns on board pushed some disabled women into the 'pro-life', anti-choice lobby, others continued a dialogue. But violence against women was not at the forefront – for example, while SAD's 1981 charter of rights makes demands for accessible environments and transport, an end to discrimination in the workplace and segregated schooling, equal state benefits and funding for disabled people's organisations, it does not raise issues of violence against disabled women.

Disabled women did start to write about their unique experiences. In 1981, Jo Campling published *Images of Ourselves*, an anthology of writing by disabled women, and in 1985 *Living Outside Inside*, a collection of writing by Susan Hannaford, a UK activist who was part of Sisters Against Disablement, was published by a US press and for the first time identified a specifically disability rights *and* feminist perspective:

> Disability is seen as a tragedy, depriving the individual of normality, and the disabled woman will be judged as unable to fulfil her 'natural' functions. (Hannaford 1985, p.75)

As discussed elsewhere in this book, that so-called lack of ability to fulfil a traditional female role is still used as a pretext for violence by partners and family members.

In 1981, the British Council of Organisations of Disabled People[7] was set up to provide a united voice for the diverse groups of disabled people, in the same year as the worldwide Disabled Peoples' International (DPI) was created, adopting the social definition, rather than the World Health Organisation's medical definitions. In 1985, disabled women activists successfully pushed for a DPI Women's Committee and DPI began to recognise the particular situation of disabled women and girls. Over 20 years later, this approach was reflected in the final text of the United Nations Convention on the Rights of Persons with Disabilities, which is discussed later in this chapter.

It is hard to find any record of specific work by UK disabled women on violence against disabled women and girls prior to the mid-1980s. The first initiatives we are aware of came from feminist disabled women's groups in the USA, Canada and countries with increasingly active groups, such as Germany. The work of organisations such as Disabled Women's Network (DAWN) Canada and DAWN Ontario, Women with Disabilities Australia (WWDA) and groups in countries such as Nicaragua and El Salvador focused on exposing the extent of the violence faced by disabled women and girls.

A 1985 survey by DAWN Canada, for example, found that violence and fear of violence were the most critical issues facing Canadian women with disabilities.[8] In 1988, DAWN Canada carried out a nationwide survey which revealed that 40 per cent of respondents had been raped, abused or assaulted; 53 per cent of women who had been disabled from birth or early childhood had been abused; women with multiple disabilities had experienced multiple abuse; and 10 per cent of women who had been abused sought help from transition houses but only half of these women were accommodated. These findings were of course mirrored 13 years later in the UK by the research discussed in this book.

With the Power of Each Breath – A Disabled Woman's Anthology was published in 1985, and became a source of inspiration to disabled women activists in the UK, revealing the possibilities for a specific disabled feminist approach (Browne, Connors and Stern 1985). The book included an article by Rebecca Grothaus on *Abuse of Women with Disabilities* in which she argued that:

> The disability rights movement does not recognise the unique concerns of disabled women. Most women in this movement perceive our disabilities as the only cause of our problems. It requires a considerable leap to recognise sex-based discrimination and identify with feminist issues like violence against women, even if we are the victims of such violence. (Browne *et al.* 1985, p.124)

This separation continues to be an issue today when violence against disabled women is often still not dealt with in a way that recognises that disabled women are women, but labels them as 'vulnerable adults' with no gender. Rebecca Grothaus went on to identify barriers faced by disabled women seeking help: most shelters (refuges) and helplines were, as some of us also noted in the UK, not accessible to disabled women. Where shelters were accessible, 'staff may be afraid to take in a battered disabled woman – they fear she won't fit in, that she can't do her share of the work, or that other women will find her depressing' (Browne *et al.* 1985, pp.125–128). She also wrote about the barriers in disabled women's heads, the shame, self-blame, fear of the courts and of retaliation, fear of re-institutionalisation and the practical difficulties of leaving a violent relationship. She went on to identify solutions such as accessible facilities and training for practitioners. These remain live issues today.

Some of these early groups have gone on to be in regular dialogue with governments, have produced resource packs for domestic violence practitioners[9] and helped improve the response to violence against disabled women. Others have disappeared altogether, but some of their former members are still active and working to keep disabled women's concerns on the political agenda.

In the UK it was not until the mid- to late 1980s that violence specifically against disabled women and girls began to appear within disability and women's rights agendas. Disabled feminist Jenny Morris wrote that:

> As with non-disabled women, disabled women face the issue of naming the violence they experience and getting others to recognise it... Feminist investigations of violence experienced by disabled women within the home would highlight abuse in *Homes* as well as *homes* and by perpetrators who are paid carers as well as those who are family members. (Morris 1996, pp.7–8)

In the same book, Sally French recounted her research into the experiences of visually impaired women in residential schools, some of which involved psychological and physical violence (French 1996). Morris also called for feminist research to 'put this under the same spotlight that has been brought to non-disabled women's lives.' She pointed out that definitions of domestic violence had been set by non-disabled women and did not include our experiences. Some of that research has now been done, but 15 years later, disabled women activists, ourselves included, are still arguing about definitions with the Home Office and domestic violence organisations. At the same time, a few disabled people's organisations began to identify the issues faced by disabled women. Mirroring Rebecca Grothaus's views several years earlier, researcher Nasa Begum wrote about the UK in 1990:

> Women with disabilities do not want to be separated or ostracised from either the disability or the women's rights movement, because it is the accumulation of the joint oppression that makes their experiences so unique. (Begum 1990)

It was – and is still in some places – difficult to have discussions about domestic violence within disabled people's organisations (DPOs). This is in part because too many DPOs are focused 'only' on disability – issues of gender, or for that matter race or sexuality, were, and still are, seen as secondary. It is also because the personal can be too painful to talk about. And we should not forget that disabled men – and indeed some women – within our communities and within our organisations are not exempt from being perpetrators of domestic violence.

One issue may also be that our organisations are reluctant, almost frightened, to take this on because we know how big the problem is: that violence against disabled people is wider than 'just' violence in the home. For example, before Disability Action Waltham Forest in East London set up its Stay Safe project (see next chapter) specifically to deal with violence against disabled people, the organisation was already supporting several individual victims of partner or family violence; once it took on a domestic violence caseworker, the floodgates opened. Several of the women (and one disabled man) Stay Safe is working with have been in violent situations for over 10 years, one for 50 years.

Significantly, all the groups (that we are aware of) that currently work on domestic violence are led by disabled women – some of whom would define themselves as feminists, some of whom have personal experience of domestic violence or institutional abuse. On the next pages are a few examples of domestic violence initiatives by disabled women and their supporters since the early 1990s. We do not claim this to be an exhaustive list.

Greater London Action on Disability Women's Project

As Brenda has already noted in her personal story, in 1992 GLAD, the umbrella organisation of disabled people's associations in London, held the first ever disabled women's conference. The conference brought disabled women from different backgrounds together and allowed us our own space to talk about our experiences and celebrate our shared identity. Concerns raised at the conference included independent living, sexuality, reproductive rights, self-advocacy, stereotyped ideas about disabled women, and having the confidence to make choices. One outcome of the conference was Brenda's appointment, in 1993, to the post of Women's Officer at GLAD – a first and, to our knowledge, unique opportunity. Brenda's job was to run the Disabled Women's Project, whose aims included putting disabled women's concerns on the agenda of disabled people's organisations, and ensuring that disabled women's concerns were heard by service planners. Issues of violence came to Brenda's attention in the course of the work, highlighting the barriers faced by disabled women in getting help. *Boadicea Disabled Women's Newsletter* was published from 1992 to 1999 and became a lively forum for debate, with a mix of personal stories and discussion articles. As part of her outreach work, Brenda contacted individual women and several disabled women's groups which existed across London at the time. It is worth noting that by the 2010s, all but one of these groups had stopped meetings and though some of the informal networks have remained, there is no longer a space for disabled women to get together.

Although funding for the Women's Officer post was short-lived, Brenda continued to promote the rights of disabled women in her role as Policy Officer at GLAD. Research into disabled women's lives, including those living in institutions, helped inform policy-makers of the issues we faced (GLAD 1997). The project events gave disabled women a voice and, for the first time, representation on key bodies such as those working on the London Domestic Violence Strategy. Although Brenda was successful in getting a first mention of disabled women in the final document and strategy, it was some years before this was to translate into practice amongst domestic violence agencies and policy bodies.

Campaigning for equality: British Council of Organisations of Disabled People (BCODP) Women's Group and Women's Committee

The BCODP Women's Group was set up in 1995 to bring together disabled women involved in the movement, liaise with other women's groups, and campaign for the rights of disabled women. Its co-chairs were Brenda Joyce and Patricia Rock. Amongst its charter of rights, published with the first newsletter, was a demand for 'the right to live in a safe and non-violent environment' (BCODP Women's Committee 1995). The charter was distributed to mainstream women's organisations as well as disability rights groups.

The group eventually became the Women's Committee of BCODP, and survived until BCODP experienced organisational problems in the first few years of the twenty-first century. UK Disabled People's Council, as the organisation is now called, has no women's committee, but has done a considerable amount of work on violence against disabled people, mainly around hate crime and human rights.

United Kingdom Disability Forum Women's Committee

Anne Pridmore, a disabled activist, was at the forefront of setting up the UK Disability Forum for European Affairs Women's Committee. Anne became involved as a representative to the Women's Committee of the European Disability Forum (see below).

With funding from Comic Relief, the UK Women's Committee organised a conference and put together an excellent resource pack for disabled women and set up a website, which for many years was the only resource available specifically for disabled women on domestic and sexual violence (UK Disability Forum 2008). The website sums up a situation which is only just beginning to change:

We need a Disabled Women's Committee because:

- Women's issues are forgotten by the disability movement

- Disability issues are forgotten by the women's movement

- Disabled women suffer the highest levels of violence and abuse, but have the fewest safe spaces.

The website is still open, and though it has not been updated since 2003, remains a useful resource.

Manifesto by Disabled Women in Europe: the European Disability Forum

Disabled women's groups, though small in numbers, have been active around domestic violence and wider women's and disabled people's rights since the 1980s in a number of European countries, including Germany, Spain and the Scandinavian countries. In 1997, soon after the European Disability Forum was set up to bring disabled people's organisations together, the *Manifesto by Disabled Women in Europe* was published. Its purpose was:

> To inform and alert women and girls with disabilities regarding their position, their rights and their responsibilities. But also to inform and alert the European Commission, the European Parliament, Member States, the European Disability Movement as well as the Women's Movement regarding the absence of gender thinking in relation to disabled women/ girls and disabled men/boys. The Manifesto is a tool for disabled women's empowerment and…should ideally form a base for political activity to improve the situation for disabled women wherever European Union policies are involved.[10]

The section on violence against women and girls is worth quoting – as a rights-based approach which nevertheless uses the concept of 'vulnerability' which we take issue with in this chapter:

> The right of disabled girls and women to live in freedom and safety should be fully recognised. Violence against disabled girls and women is a major problem and statistics show that disabled girls and women are more likely to be victims of violence because of their vulnerability. Control of their own body should be guaranteed for disabled women to protect them against physical, psychological and sexual violence. This is very important particularly for disabled women who have to stay in hospitals, rehabilitation and other institutions, and those who are unable to represent themselves.[11]

The European Disability Forum and disabled women's organisations have continued to work on violence against women and girls. A European conference on violence against disabled women was held in Falerna, Italy in 2001 and involved women from 16 countries. In 2010, the Forum issued a call for increased effort to eliminate all forms of violence against disabled women and girls. This was echoed by Equality 2025, the advisory group to the UK government on equality for disabled people, which urged the government to address this issue in the UK.

The Forum's work has influenced the European agencies to some extent. In those countries where there are effective disabled women's groups, it has led to some significant changes. But in the UK, in the absence of organised disabled women's voices, progress at government level has been slow.

The feminist 'Third Wave'

In recent years, disabled women have become regular contributors to the revived International Women's Day events, part of a rising third wave of feminist activism. Their contribution is helping to ensure that we are recognised as equal contributors to the debate and to the solutions to violence against women and girls. As speakers Michele Daley and Eleanor Lisney told participants:

> Being here today for both of us is about raising the voices of our disabled sisters. It is also about ensuring our recognition within this struggle for human rights... We all have a responsibility to ensure disabled women are recognised and respected as equals within this struggle for all of our voices to be heard – 'we are women too'! (Daley and Lisney 2010)

The work of these individuals, forums and networks is slowly helping to change the way we think about violence against disabled women and girls. They have helped introduce the issues of violence against disabled women to the policy agenda, and to increase awareness of the issues amongst disabled and women's organisations. The next step is to ensure that policy- and decision-makers take on board the changes necessary to include disabled women.

Women's Aid: change at last?

For many years, disabled women have been on the outside of domestic violence services and networks. In the last few years, as the *Making the Links* research (Hague *et al.* 2008a) reported in this book shows, there has been a shift by practitioners towards recognising that domestic violence practice cannot be inclusive without disabled women. It is to Women's Aid's credit that it recognises the gap in research and in practice and commissioned the research. Following the publication of the research, *The Survivors' Handbook* (Barron 2009) now includes a chapter which addresses the particular concerns of disabled women and lists some resources. Posters aimed at disabled women can be downloaded from the Women's Aid website (www. womensaid.org.uk). Information about which refuges provide access can be obtained from the National Domestic Violence Helpline (www.national domesticviolencehelpline.org.uk), which Women's Aid operate with Refuge.

So disability is slowly being included in the mainstream, but we have a very long way to go before domestic violence strategies are fully inclusive of disabled women, and before all refuges and support services are accessible: as the following chapter shows, there is still only one refuge in Europe that is geared to the needs of women with learning difficulties, and very few services cater for Deaf British Sign Language users. As the national coordinating body for domestic violence services, Women's Aid will continue to have a key role in making these changes happen.

Changing the law, changing society?

The Disability Discrimination Acts (1995 and 2005)

After many years of campaigning by disabled people and their allies, and many about-turns and false promises, the Disability Discrimination Act (DDA) became law in 1995. It was not the civil rights law we had campaigned for but, whatever its considerable shortcomings, it did gradually help bring about a shift from a 'special needs' approach towards a disability equality approach.

On a practical level, the first phase of the DDA slowly pushed service providers into making their services and information more accessible and, from 2004, their buildings. This has gradually impacted on domestic violence agencies. A number of women's refuges, for example, began to make provision for wheelchair users or for Deaf women, and to keep a record of that information so that disabled women could be found accommodation. But the barriers to disabled people finding out about or accessing even basic information remain. At the time of writing, for example, the National Domestic Violence Helpline and several other domestic violence helplines have no text facility for Deaf or speech-impaired callers. Sixteen years after the DDA became law, there are still woefully few accessible bed spaces across the country, and few refuges will accept Deaf women due to 'health and safety reasons' – in effect because they are not willing to pay a relatively small sum to install visual and pager systems to alert Deaf women in case of fire or other emergency. What price equality?

The most important part of the Disability Discrimination Act was the 2005 Act, which brought in a duty on public bodies to promote equality for disabled people and to produce Disability Equality Schemes. These changes gave more leverage to those of us who were pushing for change. In particular, we were able to demand to be consulted, and to request Disability Equality Impact assessments. The Metropolitan Police, for example, used this process to work with its advisers and to establish and address 'disproportionality' in the way that domestic violence against disabled women was dealt with: for example, less effective action being taken, and fewer prosecutions of perpetrators if the victim was disabled. The Metropolitan Police has begun to make changes, and there have been some examples of good practice, though spreading this across London, let alone to other police forces, will be slow.

The 2010 Equality Act

In 2010, the outgoing Labour government introduced a new Equality Act to replace the varied and sometimes inconsistent set of different equality legislation – the Race Relations Act, the Sex Discrimination Act, the DDA and directives on sexual orientation, age, maternity and gender reassignment. Like other equality groups, disabled people's organisations had mixed responses to the new Act, and to the introduction the year before of a new Commission for Equality and Human Rights to replace the old Disability Rights Commission and its sister organisations on race and gender. On the one hand, there was a fear that disability rights would be watered down further. On the other hand, the recognition that discrimination did not necessarily only take one form was welcomed by black and minority ethnic disabled people's groups and disabled lesbian, gay, bisexual and transgender groups such as Regard. The Equality Act came into force in October 2010 and covers both direct and indirect discrimination; it preserves the disability-related rights in the DDA and strengthens the rights to reasonable adjustments.

The new public sector Equality Duty came into force on 5 April 2011. The Equality Duty replaces the three previous duties on race, disability and gender, bringing them together into a single duty, and extends it to cover age, sexual orientation, religion or belief, pregnancy and maternity, and gender reassignment (EHRC 2010). The new Equality Duty requires public bodies to 'have due regard' to the need to eliminate discrimination, harassment and victimisation, advance equality of opportunity, and foster good relations in the course of developing policies and delivering services. Public bodies have to take 'proportionate action' to advance equality but no longer have to publish an Equality Scheme (which in the case of disability equality schemes had to be produced in consultation with disabled people). They now only have to publish *one or more* objectives which they reasonably think should be achieved in order to further one or more of the aims set out in the general equality duty.

At the time of writing, the coalition government is focusing efforts on 'reducing red tape' and aims to 'shift the focus of public bodies onto the delivery of equality improvements for their staff and service users, rather than have them focusing their efforts on bureaucratic processes.' While this is a laudable aim, it is those self-same processes that have pushed public sector organisations into at least having to ask questions about inequalities in their service delivery and in outcomes for different groups, including disabled women. Without published information on outcomes (for example, the actions taken against domestic violence perpetrators by police and courts), the job of campaigners will be harder. For disabled women who have only just started to engage with the state on these issues, the task will be doubly difficult.

Human rights, disabled women's rights: the United Nations Convention on the Rights of Persons with Disabilities (2007)[12]

The Convention on the Rights of Persons with Disabilities was a latecomer to the human rights framework developed within the United Nations, and it took many years for disabled people to get it agreed. Throughout, the Convention specifically recognises the specific and extensive human rights abuses faced by disabled women and girls. It is worth quoting relevant Articles.

Article 6 draws attention to the multiple discrimination faced by women and girls with disabilities:

> States Parties to take measures to ensure the full and equal enjoyment of all human rights and fundamental freedoms by women and girls with disabilities. States must ensure the full advancement and empowerment of women with disabilities.

Article 13 addresses access to justice. States which are signatories to the Convention:

> shall ensure effective access to justice for persons with disabilities on an equal basis with others, including through the provision of procedural and age-appropriate accommodations, in order to facilitate their effective role as direct and indirect participants, including as witnesses, in all legal proceedings, including at investigative and other preliminary stages.

Article 16 addresses freedom from exploitation, abuse and violence:

> States Parties shall take all appropriate legislative, administrative, social, educational and other measures to protect persons with disabilities, both within and outside the home, from all forms of exploitation, violence and abuse, including their gender-based aspects.

Article 16 places a duty on signatory countries to act to prevent exploitation, violence and abuse of disabled people by ensuring that support and assistance, services, facilities and programmes are gender- and age-sensitive, and are effectively monitored by independent authorities. Signatories to the Convention must 'put in place effective legislation and policies, including women- and child-focused legislation and policies, to ensure that instances of exploitation, violence and abuse against persons with disabilities are identified, investigated and, where appropriate, prosecuted.'

The UK government is a signatory to the Convention and can be called to account by the United Nations if it does not ensure that rights are protected. The Convention is the best tool available at present for disabled people and their allies across the world to pressure governments to take our human rights on board. It is the best tool for disabled women to use in their fight against gender-based violence and abuse.[13]

Current developments

Government strategy to end violence against women and girls

In spring 2011, as part of its national strategy to end violence against women and girls, the government published an Action Plan (HM Government 2011). The action plan acknowledges the need for collective action involving international and local government and institutions, voluntary groups and local communities (see also Chapter 8).

The principles of this vision are to:

- prevent violence from happening by challenging the attitudes and behaviours which foster it and intervening early where possible to prevent it

- provide adequate support where violence does occur

- work in partnership to obtain the best outcome for victims and their families

- take action to reduce the risk to women and girls who are victims of these crimes and ensure that perpetrators are brought to justice.

While the equality impact assessment acknowledges the findings of research, including *Making the Links*, and the views of disabled women that there is a lack of services tailored to their needs (including those for Deaf women), there appears to be no analysis of the disparity in outcomes for disabled women (HM Government 2011). Nor is there any indication that extra resources might be needed to address this disparity. A brief review of the action plan shows that disability is barely on the agenda as a specific item. The references we found are:

- Action point 9 (Attitudes, behaviours and practices): 'Explore the prevalence of violence against women and girls on vulnerable groups, and work to raise awareness both within these groups and with frontline practitioners.'

- Action point 85 (Reducing the risk for victims and rehabilitating offenders): a specific reference to women with learning difficulties as being amongst those who are more vulnerable to serious sexual assault.

There is a lack of concrete actions around most areas of diversity, but particularly around disability. We could find no specific measures to address the specific attitudinal, practical or resource barriers faced by disabled women who experience domestic violence. There is no indication of a grasp of the mismatch between safeguarding and domestic violence policies. There is no mention of the need for accessible information and resources, for example in public campaigns around domestic violence. The focus on localism, away from what is called 'national targets, rigid indicators' may possibly encourage individual examples of good practice. But without those targets, and clear guidance on good practice, disabled women will remain at the mercy of a postcode lottery as to whether their local domestic violence services are accessible and welcoming.

Equality and Human Rights Commission Inquiry

In 2011, the Equality and Human Rights Commission (EHRC) conducted an Inquiry into targeted violence against disabled people, which looked at the steps taken by public authorities to prevent and eliminate disability-related harassment (EHRC 2011b). Initially, the Commission did not plan to include domestic violence in the remit of the Inquiry but, under pressure from activists, this was changed. The Commission took evidence from a range of activists, community organisations, and statutory organisations, including the police, Crown Prosecution Service, government and local authorities. Its main focus was on change that can be effected by public sector organisations, including government, the criminal justice system and local authorities. It is hoped that the report from the Inquiry will help galvanise action on violence against disabled people, including on gender-based violence, and that the Commission will use its (limited) powers to take action where necessary.

Conclusion

In this chapter, we have explored how disabled women have been fighting to ensure that our issues and concerns as disabled women are taken on board. Although progress has been slow, the international recognition of violence against disabled women as a human rights issue has provided disabled women and their allies with a framework for tackling that violence.

Notes

1   The more extreme of these medical model solutions have been euthanasia and mass sterilisation programmes against disabled people: between 1939 and 1945 the Nazi regime sterilised 400,000 disabled people without their consent, and gassed and murdered between 200,000 and 270,000 disabled people. Forced sterilisation programmes of those deemed to be 'feeble minded' or 'lunatics' were also prevalent in Canada, the United States, Japan, Sweden and many other countries, in some cases up till the 1970s.

2   A number of other disabled women activists were also campaigning for the inclusion of disabled women and had been doing so for much longer than me. Many of these women's contributions have never been acknowledged. Names that spring to mind are Anne Pridmore, Jenny Morris, Rachel Hurst, Jane Campbell, Ruth Bashall, Kirsten Hearn, Val Stein, Simone Aspis, Frances Hasler, Patricia Rock, Nasa Begum, Pauline McGowan, Millie Hill, Anne Novis, Menghi Mulchandani, Kath Gillespie-Sells, Pam Moffatt. There are and were many more. Some of these women are no longer with us. We do remember you and we won't forget your contributions.

3   LANGUID: Lesbians and Gays Unite in Disability, a national network of disabled lesbians and gay men was founded in the late 1980s. It was replaced in the early 1990s by REGARD (see www.regard.org.uk).

4   Audre Lorde (1934–1992) was a black feminist lesbian poet whose writings inspired a generation of activists. Her Cancer Journals chronicle her life with cancer.

5   Laura Hershey (1962–2010) was a US feminist, disability human rights activist, writer, poet and blogger (see www.laurahershey.com).

6   We could not include here all the work by disabled women in the UK around violence against disabled women and girls – our history is yet to be written, and too much of it is lost. We have, however, tried to give a flavour of the work of some of the disabled women and their organisations who have worked to make this world a safer and more equal place for their disabled sisters; their work has so rarely been acknowledged by movements for women's or disabled people's rights.

7   Now United Kingdom Disabled People's Council (see www.ukdpc.net).

8   Source: DAWN Ontario, available at www.dawn.thot.net.

9   In the 1990s, WWDA (1999) produced an excellent resource guide: 'More Than Just A Ramp' – A Guide for Women's Refuges to Develop Disability Discrimination Act Action Plans. See next chapter for more details.

10 Manifesto by Disabled Women in Europe. Adopted in Brussels on 22 February 1997 by the European Disability Forum Working Group on Women and Disability. Launched in the European Parliament on 4 December 1999 (see UK Disability Forum 2011).

11 Ibid. Section 7.1.

12 For the full text and an explanation of the Convention, see Equality and Human Rights Commission (2011a).

13 The United Kingdom Disabled People's Council has now set up Disability Rights Watch UK, a project that aims to ensure that disabled people and their organisations are actively involved in monitoring disabled people's human rights in the UK (see www. disabilityrightswatchuk.org). Though the project has no specific gender focus, it will allow UKDPC to put together further evidence of violence against disabled men and women.

Chapter 6

Nothing About Us Without Us

Policy and Practice

Ruth Bashall and Brenda Ellis

This chapter challenges current thinking about key issues which arise when considering how to address domestic violence and disabled women: gender, disability and 'vulnerability', and the definition of domestic violence. Elsewhere in this book, others consider the practical barriers for disabled women in getting support and justice. Here we consider how understanding the political and social context of the lives of disabled women might help to address those barriers and shape good practice. We look at some different approaches to good practice, and what the principles might be.

Understanding the violence

Unravelling the complex relationship between patriarchy, a disabling society, and other forms of discrimination and marginalisation such as homophobia and racism is essential to understanding the *solutions* to violence against disabled women. As feminists, we subscribe to the idea that violence against women and girls is a specific aspect of gender discrimination – domestic and sexual violence are a means of control and exercising power, and are a consequence of misogyny and patriarchal structures. We know that violence against lesbian, gay or transgender people within societies or families is also a result of that same set of patriarchal attitudes and punishes anyone who does not 'fit' the established pattern of gender roles. But we also know there are no easy explanations, and that violence happens within lesbian or gay relationships, and that some men experience domestic violence.

We define patriarchy as attitudes and systems that put women at a disadvantage, that relegate us to the status of secondary human being. It is about power relations between men and women as social groupings and as individuals. It is also about valuing strength and a particular kind of autonomy. Disabled people – men or women – rarely fit into that model of patriarchy.

As *disabled* feminists, we know that for disabled women, whatever our ethnicity or sexuality, there is a specific *disability* aspect to the violence we face. We are aware that disabled men are more likely than non-disabled men to experience domestic or other forms of violence. We know that there are cultural, religious and sexuality aspects to domestic violence. So we know that domestic violence is gender-based, but not only gender-based. But how does this impact on how we address violence against disabled women and girls?

There is common ground. Feminist concepts of oppression and of the 'personal is political' are not so very different from the social model of disability, which argues that the personal is political when it results in oppression and discrimination. To understand violence against disabled women, we have to understand how the power relations that exist between non-disabled and disabled people affect us all, and in particular the position of disabled women in society.

Violence against disabled people: marginalisation or inclusion?

As already noted, we live in a society where, until recently, solutions to 'what to do with disabled people' involved institutionalisation, often for life, and the denial of human rights, and concomitant physical, sexual and psychological abuse. Unless we could 'cope' in the community, non-disabled professionals and our families had all the power – they were the 'disability experts' and could make decisions about whether we lived or died, whether we went to school with other children, or lived at home or in an institution, had relationships, were able to access training or were allowed to work. We were infantilised, and not in charge of our destiny. Sometimes we were killed, or sterilised so we did not reproduce. It is worth remembering that it was not just the Nazis who saw disabled people as 'useless eaters' – alongside Winston Churchill, Marie Stopes, a feminist who campaigned for the right of (married) women to control their own bodies, was a fervent eugenicist who argued for compulsory sterilisation of 'the insane, the feeble-minded...' as well as 'half-castes' (Stopes 1920).

As set out in the previous chapter, it is only since the early 1980s that disabled people have begun to identify disability not as an individual flaw, in body or mind, but as social oppression against people who happen to have an impairment. The disabled people's movement and its allies have helped bring about considerable change – not least that many disabled people now live independently in the community. In the UK and in some other countries[1] in the 1980s and 1990s, many people were moved out of long-stay institutions. Society no longer automatically looks to institutionalisation or hospitalisation as the solution for anyone with a mental health issue or learning difficulty. Housing is more accessible, with national minimum standards. There is greater freedom of movement for disabled people (in urban areas at least), and a greater proportion of disabled children and young people is in mainstream education alongside their peers.[2] Attitudes to disabled people are changing, with disabled people more included and accepted as part of the mainstream (Mencap 2011).[3] The introduction of direct payments for social care in the 1990s removed many of the restrictions on the lives of those of us who need everyday help: being able to choose who assists you with personal care or living your life removes some (though not all) of the opportunities for abuse and violence against disabled people. And for a few years before cuts began to bite, parts at least of the social care system accepted that a disabled person living with a partner or family member did not necessarily have to depend on them, but could have a care package that would allow them to be an equal member of that family.

Progress, however, is not straightforward. These changes have not reached all disabled people. Even in wealthy countries such as the UK, many disabled people get no practical help even when they need it, and have no option but to depend on their families or charitable organisations, or to live lives of extreme social isolation. There has been an increase in the number of older disabled people living in institutional care in recent years, and a move towards more oppressive treatment of people with mental health distress. Levels of violence against disabled people remain extremely high, whether they live in the community or in institutions. A culture of risk-minimisation within social services departments has pulled in the opposite direction to the movement for independent living, with a focus on risk minimisation and protection, and the over-formalisation of independent living into 'personalisation', where it is not always clear who is in control. Above all, poverty and deprivation continue to go hand in hand with disability.

At time of writing, the Conservative–Liberal Democrat coalition is in the process of making drastic cuts to benefits and social care, as further discussed in the next two chapters, and moving away from independent living towards an 'interdependency' model. This may leave disabled people in a position of increased dependency on their families or on the goodwill of communities, and increase the potential for domestic violence and abuse. Gains made since the early 1990s are under threat not only from those cuts in services, but from the hounding of disabled people by governments and the media as cheats and scroungers – at the same time as the numbers of attacks on disabled people are rising, and disabled people's organisations which provided support for independent living are under threat.

Violence is normal

We still live in a world where violence against disabled women and men is commonplace and often goes unchallenged: infanticide of disabled newborns, denial of medical care because someone's life is judged to be 'not worth living', everyday violence in state institutions, and hiding disabled adults and children in the family home out of fear and shame. Our world does not value the lives of disabled people. Is the birth of a disabled child welcomed, or is it still viewed as a tragedy for the family and for society? On the one hand, an increasing number of parents are rejecting that idea and fighting the disability hatred which they and their children experience; on the other hand, the media is full of stories about 'mercy killings' of disabled people.[4] We have found ourselves asking how many of these are, in fact, domestic violence in disguise? Is a disabled life worth less? After all, if you kill a 'normal' person, it's a crime of homicide. If you kill a disabled person, particularly one who has a so-called 'severe disability', you are committing an act of mercy, releasing the disabled person from a life that others consider not worth living, and releasing yourself or your family from the 'burden of caring'. A parent who kills their disabled child may be seen as deserving sympathy, whereas a parent who murders their non-disabled child is labelled a monster and faces social rejection and the wrath of the tabloid press, whatever the pressures on them. These are complex issues, but all too often public attitudes, and in some cases those of the criminal justice system, are altered by that word 'disabled'.

The view that the victim is not quite human and is worthless was expressed by one of the young perpetrators of the murder of Brent Martin[5] who said in court, 'I'm not going down for that muppet' (Scope/Disability Now/UK Disabled People's Council 2008).[6] The judge in this case (and many other similar cases) failed to impose the additional sentence allowed in law[7] if a crime can be shown to be motivated by hostility towards the victim because of their disability.

A 2010 report by Anne Novis for the UK Disabled People's Council found that 'disabled people suffer multiple and continuous violations through the systems, structures and attitudes of society.' UKDPC identified 'a reluctance by professionals concerned to acknowledge the inherent disablism in society' (Novis 2010, p.1).

The UKDPC report showed a widespread pattern of often extreme violence against disabled people in the UK. As disabled feminist Katharine Quarmby wrote:

> Casual disablism permeates our society. The widespread belief that it is legitimate to treat disabled people differently and to routinely deny them equal access to things that others take for granted, creates an environment where disability hate crime can exist without being recognised or challenged. Disablist attitudes are still the norm, they are so entrenched that when disablism escalates into hate crime, few people are able or willing to recognise it for what it is. (Novis 2010, p.32)

The UKPDC report found evidence[8] of 68 killings of disabled people in the UK between August 2007 and July 2010. Twenty-nine of the 68 victims were disabled women. Twenty-one of these murders occurred between January and July 2010. In the same period in 2010, 317 attacks or incidents were recorded in the press. These included 68 incidents of 'carer abuse', 44 of them in care homes, 30 rapes or sexual assaults and seven domestic violence crimes – it is likely that the latter figure is low because most domestic violence cases do not get into the papers, and because recording of whether a victim is a disabled person is unreliable. The experience of Francesca Hardwick, a woman with learning difficulties, and her mother Fiona Pilkington made the national headlines. After years of severe harassment by local youths and a complete failure to act by Leicestershire police (see *Guardian* 2009), Fiona Pilkington set fire to their car with herself and Francesca Hardwick in it.

These disability hate crime cases show a striking resemblance to those involving domestic violence – repeat offences, in some cases multiple perpetrators, humiliation, excessive violence, degrading treatment, and of course a lack of action by the authorities (Brookes 2010).

Talking about the violence

Language can both reflect and influence how we think about an issue – and for this reason, Stephen Brookes, a disability rights activist who works on hate crime, recommends that:

> We should avoid saying:
>
> - 'Motiveless crime' – if we mean the motive is not known or is not clear to us.
>
> - 'There is no evidence' – if we mean there is insufficient evidence.

- 'Vulnerable victim' – when we mean someone was in a vulnerable situation that was exploited by the offender (as opposed to, for example, the use of the word in the statutory context.

- 'Bullying' – use of this word understates the seriousness of incidents that often involve intimidation, persecution, terror, fear, harassment, i.e. behaviours amounting to criminal offences. Even 'mere' ridicule, mimicking, exclusion can amount to causing serious harassment, alarm or distress, particularly if repeated.

- 'Has a mental age of' – comparison of an adult person with a child is often considered to be demeaning and unhelpful. Better practice is a reference to the person's level of social functioning and understanding.

(Brookes 2010, p.6)

Violence against disabled women: living in an unequal world

If the everyday, 'public' violence goes unreported, unpunished and unstopped, how much more likely is it that violence within the home or a 'home' will also go unreported, undetected, unpunished and will continue for years? If a disabled life has less value than a non-disabled life, how much less the worth of a disabled *female* life? Domestic violence is an expression of hatred and contempt. It is about control. The majority of disabled women across the world are not in control of their lives:

> Women and girls with disabilities live at the intersection of gender and disability bias. As a consequence, they experience higher rates of violence and lower rates of service access than their non-disabled peers. (Jennings 2003)

Assuming an identity as a disabled woman means recognising our unique experience. And that is not always a happy one: disabled women across the world have fewer choices, less autonomy than almost anyone else. It is not possible to consider violence against disabled women without understanding and addressing such inequalities, and outside of a human rights framework.

Disabled women, if they survive childhood, have even fewer choices in their lives in terms of education, employment or independent income, relationships, motherhood and life opportunities than their non-disabled sisters. Disabled People's International (2010), the international network of organisations run by disabled people lists some of the inequalities faced by disabled women and girls:

- Disabled women face a heightened risk of gender-based violence.

- Literacy rates amongst disabled women globally may be as low as 1 per cent.

- Mortality rates amongst disabled girls are higher even than amongst disabled boys due to neglect, poor access to medical care and reduced access to food and other resources.

- Disabled girls are more likely to be institutionalised than disabled boys.

- Disabled women have significantly lower levels of access to reproductive health care services than non-disabled women.

- Disabled women and girls living in institutions experience higher rates of physical and sexual abuse, and in some cases face abuse rates double those of disabled women and girls living in the community.

While not all the factors are as unequal in the UK, they still impact on the likelihood of a disabled woman being a victim of domestic or institutional violence. In 2011, there are still many disempowered disabled women, many of them living segregated lives. Separate schools, classes at college for people with learning difficulties, day centres, supported housing and hospitals are not usually settings in which rights feature on the agenda or where domestic violence is discussed. Women of all ages are the majority residents or users of such settings. It is still the case that for many disabled people a home is in fact a 'home', where the risk of violence or abuse from staff members, fellow residents or volunteers is high. In our experience, there remains a marked reluctance on the part of special schools to discuss issues of sexuality, let alone power issues within relationships. Disabled women are also more likely to be isolated within the home, less likely to be in paid work, and more likely to depend on family members for assistance. It is also still very much the case that disabled women and girls, even those who have contact with disabled people's self-advocacy or campaigning groups, are more likely to subscribe to traditional gender roles. This is in part because disabled women have in the past been denied any form of personal expression as women. Women with learning difficulties or high support needs have been especially affected by this – while now it is acknowledged that they have some level of sexuality, their sexuality is often infantilised, or kept within the confines of a very conventional heterosexuality. All these factors combine to makes women and girls ill-equipped to deal with unwanted sexual attention, let alone power issues within relationships, and to have the confidence to leave a violent relationship.

Defining domestic violence

How we define a problem sets the context for solutions. Definitions of what is and is not domestic violence have changed over the years, as society's understanding has moved on, and as campaigners have pushed for a more comprehensive definition that reflects the diverse reality of women's and men's experiences of violence. Like black women in previous decades, disabled women have issues with the way in which definitions of domestic violence fail to include the reality of our lives.

The Association of Chief Police Officers (ACPO) defines domestic violence as:

> Any incident of threatening behaviour, violence or abuse (psychological, physical, sexual, financial or emotional) between adults, aged 18 and over, who are or have been *intimate* partners or family members, regardless of gender and sexuality. (Family members are defined as mother, father, son, daughter, brother, sister and grandparents, whether directly related, in-laws or step-family.) (ACPO and NPIA 2008, p.7; emphasis added)

The Women's Aid definition is not substantially different (as noted in Chapter 1):

> Domestic violence is physical, sexual, psychological or financial violence that takes place within an *intimate or family-type relationship* and that forms a pattern of coercive and controlling behaviour. This can include forced marriage and so-called 'honour crimes'. Domestic violence may include a range of abusive behaviours, not all of which are in themselves inherently 'violent'. (Women's Aid 2007; emphasis added)

Both of these definitions are now widely accepted and are gender and sexuality neutral. And although the Women's Aid definition encompasses a wider definition of family, both assume that the perpetrator is a 'family' member. Indeed, in Chapter 1, the need for these definitions to be expanded to better take account of disabled women's experiences was noted. Along with other disabled women and some disabled people's organisations, we have been arguing for some years that current definitions fail to take account of two critical sources of violence for disabled women (and men):

- Violence and abuse by paid or voluntary carers in someone's home or private life.

- Violence that happens in a residential or semi-residential setting but is still 'home' to the victim.

Those settings are domestic. Those relationships, while in some ways formal, are also intimate. So why are they not considered to be domestic violence and dealt with as such? Why is an abusive relationship with a partner, or with a family member who acts as an unpaid carer (which would be covered by the domestic violence definition), considered to be any more intimate than an equally abusive relationship with someone who is a paid worker, or even a volunteer, who has got to know the disabled person? Boundaries in such situations are fluid, and the perpetrator may be closer to and know more about the disabled person than actual family members. Currently, abuse by a paid or unpaid 'carer' would be dealt with as a 'Safeguarding Adults' matter. The Metropolitan Police in its policy on Safeguarding Adults defines such situations as follows:

> A single or repeated act or lack of appropriate action occurring within any relationship where there is *an expectation of trust* (which can include a relative, carer or service provider) which causes harm or distress (physical, psychological, financial, sexual or neglect) to a vulnerable adult. (London Metropolitan Police 2009; emphasis added)

But within families is there not also an expectation of trust? The Metropolitan Police protocols at least recognise that a safeguarding situation can also be a domestic violence one, but these two definitions point to confusion about the situation of disabled people. Yet all of the above violence and abuse are about abuse of power – whether by partners, family members or paid or unpaid carers and assistants.

One reason for this confusion is that disabled people who need assistance are placed in a context which non-disabled people do not experience: any violence is not public as in hate crime, not intimate in the sense defined by conventional definitions of domestic violence, but perpetrated in private space, someone's home, by external people who perform intimate tasks for us. This applies whether the home in question is one's own home, or a group 'home' or a larger residential facility.

Personal care is the most intimate, but domestic tasks, help with daily living, shopping, monitoring medication, help with getting around or with managing money, and ironically, help with keeping safe are all intimate in the sense that they are one-to-one, involving the person who is assisting knowing some level of personal information about the disabled woman, her life, her finances, her impairment. If the woman is isolated and unsupported, the risk to her of being financially, physically or otherwise abused is greater:

The problem for us is how do you define 'intimate' and domestic. How intimate is my relationship with the person who helped me out of the bath this morning, assisted me to get dressed and so on? I reckon that is pretty intimate. Even if I were using an agency, this is still an intimate task, in my own home – a domestic situation. If I live in a residential home, it is still my home and the workers who perform essential tasks for me are intimates, whether I like it or not. And if that worker is a family member or friend who does not live with me but acts as a 'carer', paid or unpaid, it is still an intimate, domestic situation. If that 'carer', or 'helper' or even 'personal assistant', tries to force feed me, or denies me food, or abuses me financially, or is physically violent to me – to me, that breach of trust in my own home is domestic violence. How I will experience it will not in many ways be different from violence from a partner or family member. (Bashall 2006)

So we would argue that current definitions of domestic violence fail to listen to the person who should be at the core of the issue, the victim/survivor herself. The definitions do not reflect the reality of many disabled women's lives.

We of course recognise the need to protect other potential victims: where domestic violence is perpetrated by a non-family member, there are wider implications, particularly the need to ensure that further abuse or violence is not perpetrated against any other disabled person with whom the perpetrator is able to gain employment or trust. But established domestic violence processes already allow the identification of repeat offenders who target one woman after another to subject them to violence and abuse, so why two different procedures?

It is already known that levels of domestic violence are much higher than reported incidents, which show one woman in four being a victim of domestic violence in her lifetime. We know from the research described in this book that up to 50 per cent of disabled women have experience of domestic violence.[9] Many others have experienced sexual abuse, hate crime, constant harassment and bullying, as evidenced by the Equality and Human Rights Commission's own research (EHRC 2009). How much higher would those statistics be if the physical, psychological, financial and emotional abuse and violence perpetrated against disabled women and men by non-family so-called 'carers' in their own homes, or by people working in 'homes' were to be included, or if violence against people who are deemed to be 'vulnerable adults' were to be included?

Vulnerable adult abuse or domestic violence?

In the days before feminism, and before we came to see violence against women and girls as a political and societal issue, building on our discussions in the last chapter, we used to talk about 'vulnerable victims' of domestic and sexual violence. We talked about 'battered wife syndrome' as a psychological condition, a flaw in the individual 'victim'. Society looked for an explanation of the violence in the characteristics of its victims: certain types of women were seen as almost predestined victims of male violence because of their social status or their occupation – poor women, sex workers, women who did not conform to what was expected. The misogynistic attitudes towards violence against sex workers, or women who have been raped when drunk, or towards so-called 'honour-based violence' show there is still work to be done. But by and large we understand that most domestic violence happens not because women are willing or inevitable victims but because of patriarchy – men choose to rape or perpetrate violence in a society which privileges male power.

However, society (and policy-makers) still sees most violence against disabled women and men not as domestic violence, or hate crime, but as a result of some innate 'vulnerability' caused by their impairment. In other words, society takes a medical model approach to violence against disabled people, a separate 'special needs' approach. It uses a 'safeguarding vulnerable adults' approach. In our view and that of many disabled women, this approach is a major barrier to progress. We propose an alternative social model approach, where solutions to domestic violence are about an inclusive approach to prevention, support and services.

Under pressure from disabled people, and after many deaths, there is a level of public debate about, for example, disability-related hate crime. But disabled people are having to work hard to challenge the terms of this debate: society persists in calling violence against many disabled people 'vulnerable adult abuse' and giving it a different status and recognition, not to mention different processes for tackling it, most of which do not work. It is who we are, our innate characteristics, that explain why we may be abused in the street, on public transport, in our homes. It is as if the suffering of the victim was in some way less because she or he is in need of protection, or is different. We do not treat 'vulnerable adult abuse' as a crime but as a protection issue for the victim. We rarely prosecute rape, torture or domestic violence against people who are seen as vulnerable. So it continues to happen.

We will use two examples, both of which relate to the experiences of women we know.

If a woman who has learning difficulties is 'befriended' by a man who subsequently moves in with her, abuses her and assaults her, society considers that this happened because she is too trusting and does not understand boundaries. And the perpetrator is likely to have focused on this woman because she is socially isolated and powerless and because he knows that no one will challenge him. In fact it is her situation of isolation and discrimination that makes her vulnerable, not her impairment in itself.

Similarly, if a woman is half-starved and left to sit all day with no stimulation, her family deny her social interaction and the opportunity to go outside her home – that is domestic violence. But if we add that this woman's home was a residential home, that she was disabled, and that her short-term memory was impaired, is it still domestic violence? Is it about her family 'doing their best' for her? Or does it become abuse of a 'vulnerable adult'? If the latter, the violence against this woman is no longer a crime and the remit of the criminal justice system, but a social services 'safeguarding' issue subject to endless case conferences and ineffective regulators, and the woman herself is not involved.

This 'safeguarding' model is especially ineffective when dealing with institutional abuse; but it is hardly more effective in dealing with violence and abuse against people in the community or in their own homes. Government and practitioners are going some way towards recognising the ineffectiveness of this approach, which is based on the national *No Secrets* guidance (Department of Health and Home Office 2005), but have yet to recognise that the label 'vulnerable' in itself is a problem. While procedures for tackling abuse against 'vulnerable adults' are being tightened, they do not get to the heart of the problem.

The Equality and Human Rights Commission's research has a key part to play in challenging this concept of innate vulnerability:

> The discourse around the issues surrounding disabled people's experiences of targeted violence and hostility needs to be reframed. The emphasis on help and protection (protectionism) underpinning much of existing policy and legislation should be replaced by a focus on justice and redress (rights-based paradigm). (EHRC 2009, p.viii)

The EHRC's research argued that policy and practice should move away from the idea of vulnerable groups of individuals to one of *situational vulnerability*, which the EHRC defines as:

> An institutional, family or support situation that makes the person vulnerable because they have no knowledge, choice or power. (EHRC 2009)

This approach argues, in other words, that disabled women are disempowered by their situation. For disabled women experiencing domestic and gender-based violence, being disempowered means:

- not knowing or believing another life is possible
- not being able to access alternatives
- knowing there are alternatives but fearing that change will mean things get worse.

As in the first example above, a situation of vulnerability will be exploited by a perpetrator who may target a disabled woman. This is about making the perpetrator accountable – as someone who is committing a crime and abuse of human rights.

The current protectionist model, or other people knowing what is best for us, also has an impact on disclosure. Disabled women fear talking about the personal because as disabled women, we and our bodies and minds have always been public or medical public property. Women do not want to expose their personal lives further, and as the *Making the Links* research shows, they fear the consequences of speaking out. Even the possibility of being institutionalised, or of being forced to return to the 'care' of family, is a considerable deterrent. So staying in a relationship that is violent may be preferable to living in an institution; disabled women who have never known anything else may believe that a life of violence and powerlessness is their lot, and cannot be changed. And even if they think otherwise, where do they go? As this research shows, the barriers faced by disabled women, whatever their impairment, in getting help and justice are considerable.

The EHRC research also proposed a model around 'layers of influence' to understand the situation of disabled people:

> This recognises that experiences and outcomes are not simply determined by the characteristics by any one individual, group or organisation but by extremely complex interactions across and within these entities. (EHRC 2009, p.91)

For most non-disabled women, the key contacts are with families including partners, friends, their local community and work or educational bodies. For disabled women there are added layers of people and institutions (paid or unpaid carers, social care and mental health professionals, day centre staff) who are involved in their lives, have an enormous amount of personal information about the woman herself and whose duty to protect also gives them power over the disabled woman herself. It is hardly surprising that disabled women in these circumstances are reluctant to report minor levels of harassment from outsiders, let alone domestic violence. Solutions will need to be designed that take account of these power relations and in fact move away from a protectionist model to one based on human rights.

The 'burden of caring'?

At the launch of Disability Action Waltham Forest's 'Stay Safe' project on domestic violence and hate crime, a member of the audience asked if disabled people were the victims of domestic violence because of the 'burden of care' – the pressure on 'carers' who were left unsupported to deal with their disabled 'dependants' – and whether this created a situation of potential violence.

There is no question that sometimes, *some* people lash out under pressure. But there is a significant difference between one-off violence under pressure and the sustained, daily physical, psychological or other violence which most victims of domestic violence experience. More to the point, would we still be asking that question if the victim were not a disabled person? Would we feel sympathy for a man who snaps because his 'nagging wife' pushed him too far? Of course some courts and media still do express such views, but the prevailing view in the twenty-first century in the UK is that the only appropriate response to the question is that 'domestic violence is never acceptable'.[10]

Domestic violence and safeguarding: the same issue?

The narrow definition of domestic violence, and the separation between domestic violence and safeguarding procedures, determine how agencies deal with violence against disabled women and impact on the solutions or options offered.

Radford and Hester (2006) use a three 'planets' concept to show the disconnection between domestic violence and child protection, in situations where a domestic violence victim has children.[11] This model could be usefully adapted to describe the relationship between domestic violence against disabled women: Planet A is domestic violence, Planet B adult protection, and Planet C action and solutions. At present, there is little ideological or operational overlap between Planet A, agencies that deal with domestic violence, and Planet B, those that deal with adult safeguarding. Actions and solutions are different. Even with agencies that deal with both, such as police Community Safety Units (CSUs), there are still two 'planets' in the minds of professionals.

On the one hand we have established domestic violence processes that keep the woman at the centre, work with her, help keep her safe, support her to get on with her life and regain her independence. They also recognise that in some situations the woman may choose to return to a violent situation. These procedures[12] are, by and large, transparent – statutory and voluntary agencies work together within a common framework, talk to each other and share information, sometimes challenge each other, and take action. They often lead to successful prosecution of the perpetrator. Domestic (and sexual) violence is generally recognised as something which society wants to stop. In spite of ambiguous attitudes demonstrated by a substantial minority of the public towards violence against women and girls, there are clear penalties. The law sees this as a crime and does not (generally) hold the woman responsible for the violence that has happened to her. Whatever its failings, the law gives a clear message to perpetrators that they will be punished. Though these procedures still have to be improved in order to take account of the particular situation of disabled women, by and large they save lives and allow the victim to get the best support possible (Social Care Institute for Excellence 2011). (Principles of good practice are discussed later in this chapter.)

On the other hand, Safeguarding Adults procedures focus on protection, minimising harm and social care solutions, including in some cases institutional ones. They rarely prioritise the victim regaining her independence. Though procedures are gradually being tightened in the light of a number of institutional failures, the national *No Secrets* guidance is just that – non-statutory guidance which carries no legal weight. Procedures happen with little meaningful involvement of the victim[13] and behind closed doors, led by social services rather than the police. Local advocacy agencies can be invited, but there is no obligation for them to be involved unless they are representing the disabled person. Sometimes the process is about ticking boxes. Where action is taken, it can be ineffective, and relatively rarely leads to prosecution. If the disabled woman reports an incident or incidents and is believed, an investigation takes place, but the police may not always be involved. We have noticed a marked unwillingness to see family carers of disabled people as potential abusers. Agency or residential home staff who are accused of abuse, neglect, violence, or in some cases rape, will be suspended. There is a real risk that they will in the meantime go on to temporary work elsewhere via an agency and continue the abuse – not all agencies do thorough Criminal Records Bureau (CRB) checks immediately, and the accusation may not appear on a CRB check while it is being investigated. Because in many cases the victim is seen as an 'unreliable witness', for example if they are non-verbal or have learning difficulties or mental health issues, the investigation may lead to nothing. There may also be a reluctance on the part of some privatised agencies to admit that their staff may be abusing people.

These safeguarding processes have in many instances failed to protect disabled people from abuse, violence and murder.[14] In some cases they have meant long-term cover-up of abuse. Violence by partners and other family members against people who are deemed to be vulnerable is not always treated as domestic violence. So a crime is not recognised as a crime and is not accorded the same resources or importance in terms of prevention. This gives a clear message to disabled women and men that violence against us is not taken seriously.

We have spoken to disabled people who have 'been through' Safeguarding Adults procedures, and none have felt they had any control over the process. Indeed, the fear of institutionalisation, or even of social services involvement, is a deterrent to reporting abuse. So the violence and abuse continue.

In summary, it is clear to us that a new approach is needed, which merges domestic violence and 'safeguarding of vulnerable adults' procedures so that police, statutory services and support services accord equal importance and resources to both domestic violence and 'vulnerable adult abuse', whoever the victim is. If disabled women are to be safe, this gap must be bridged and a single approach adopted. In the next section we look at how this might work.

What does good practice look like?

The second half of this chapter looks at what good practice might look like – based on a social model, and an inclusive approach that values the lives of all women, disabled and non-disabled alike. First we look at some examples of provision that meets the needs of disabled women. Later, we look at the principles which, in our view, should govern good practice.

The following are examples of initiatives which have attempted to tackle violence against disabled women, either separately or within existing projects. All of these projects are locally based, but have useful lessons for domestic violence work across the countries of the UK.

Beverley Lewis House: from peer support group to formal provision

In 1991 in East London, a diverse group of disabled and non-disabled women, most of whom were women with learning difficulties, came together in a group called the Powerhouse (POWER = Protecting Ourselves, Women with Learning Difficulties for Equal Rights). They began to talk about the physical, sexual and psychological abuse they had suffered, how it made them feel, and about not feeling welcomed or included in mainstream refuges. One of their early leaflets said:

Women with learning disabilities:

- Get attacked in their homes, at day centres, in the streets
- Get frightened
- Get angry
- Want support
- Want women's groups for themselves
- Want to be believed
- Have a right to be believed and heard

We are breaking the silence and we demand a safe house for women with learning disabilities.

The group's hard work paid off and funding was found for a housing association to build a refuge from scratch. The women worked with the architects to design the safe house, which provides women with privacy and space (each has her own room, bathroom and kitchen, and two of the six bedrooms are fully wheelchair accessible, while the others have level access). The safe house provides sleep-in accommodation for staff, as women staying at the safe house need 24-hour support – and someone on hand to talk to at any time, something that is essential for women with learning difficulties. The group decided to name the house after Beverley Lewis, a black woman with learning difficulties who had died of neglect because of the failure of social services to support her mother (who was also disabled) and family as her carers. Although the women from the Powerhouse are no longer involved directly with Beverley Lewis House, the Powerhouse group continues as a peer support group for women with learning difficulties.

Beverley Lewis House opened in 1995 and is now a national service run by East Living, an organisation which provides support and homes to people with learning difficulties and mental health issues, and to older people. Beverley Lewis House is a refuge specifically for women with learning difficulties, mainly those who also have additional support needs. It provides 24-hour support to women who have survived domestic violence, prostitution, institutional abuse, rape and other forms of abuse. The project also runs workshops for its residents so they can learn 'the life skills they need to protect themselves and live more independently, covering topics including personal safety planning, relationship management and budgeting' (see the Beverley Lewis House website at www.east-thames.co.uk).

Beverley Lewis House remains the only refuge in the UK – and in Europe – specifically for women with learning difficulties. It was set up because existing services discriminated against women with learning difficulties. Services such as Beverley Lewis House are likely to continue to be needed alongside mainstream domestic violence services, but this does not let so-called mainstream services off the hook from providing inclusive services, not least because they have a moral and legal duty to do so.

Leeds Inter-Agency Project (now the Leeds Domestic Violence Team)

Set up in 1990, the Leeds Inter-Agency Project (Women & Violence) is one of the small number of projects which have led the way in working in partnership with disabled women. LIAP was set up to develop a multi-agency approach to improve the safety of women and their children experiencing violence from men they know. As part of its work, LIAP worked with a group of disabled women survivors to produce a training pack for workshops on issues for disabled women (LIAP 2002). Aimed both at disabled women and at workers in domestic violence agencies, the pack is called DISBELIEF:

Disabled women

Ignored

Segregated

Blamed

Entitled to

Live

Independently

Empowered

Free from violence

The pack is an education tool aimed at raising awareness and at promoting good practice. It includes a video of four disabled women talking about their experiences and the barriers they faced in seeking help. It includes some useful guidance for practitioners about supporting disabled women. There are further examples of their work in Chapters 8 and 9.

Glasgow: women's organisations and disabled people's organisations working together

Glasgow has a well-structured network of women's organisations working together as part of the Glasgow Violence Against Women partnership. Wise

Women is a feminist organisation set up in 1994 to 'address women's fears and experiences of crime and violence'. It provides personal safety and confidence-building courses, as well as providing support and information and challenging male violence. The partnership is taking action to improve services to disabled and Deaf women across Glasgow. Glasgow's Disability Alliance is a membership-led organisation of disabled people and groups in Glasgow which 'act as a collective, representative voice of disabled people, promoting equality, rights and social justice.'

THE DAISIE PROJECT

Wise Women, after consultation with the Glasgow Disability Alliance, was successful in getting funding from the Scottish government's Violence Against Women Service Development Fund for work with disabled women. The two-year Daisie Project was set up 'to offer dignified, respectful and equal inclusion to the organisation's service specifically for women with physical and sensory impairments.' As part of its work, it carried out a survey of disabled women's experiences of violence, abuse and discrimination, including domestic violence. Wise Women worked with Glasgow Disability Alliance to identify a core group of women to steer the project. The research report (2010) shows that:

- Almost three-quarters (73%) of disabled women surveyed had experienced domestic abuse.

- 23 per cent of disabled woman had been raped.

- 43 per cent of disabled women reported sexual assault.

- Personal care, such as bathing, toilet assistance and eating, were regularly withdrawn. Not being allowed contact with others and the 'silent treatment' from abusers were also reported.

- In many cases, women were too scared to leave their abuser behind because they relied on them for care.

The research used interesting involvement methods – not only two consultation events, but six personal safety and confidence-building courses, which helped participants to network and gain information and confidence.

DEAF WOMEN AGAINST VIOLENCE

Deaf Women Against Violence, a small group of Deaf women, and Wise Women have produced a British Sign Language DVD[15] (with spoken English voice-over) on violence against women in partnership with Deaf women and with Strathclyde police and other agencies. Deaf women talk about their stories, and the pack provides details of text and other accessible means of contacting key support services. This is one of very few resources accessible to Deaf women that we have found, and could easily be duplicated elsewhere.

A user-led, integrated approach to violence against disabled people: Stay Safe Project, Disability Action Waltham Forest, London[16]

In 1995, Disability Action Waltham Forest (DAWF) (then Waltham Forest Association of Disabled People) was the first disabled people's organisation to commission research into domestic violence against disabled women. Fifteen years later, DAWF received funding from the Equality and Human Rights Commission for a project to work on hate crime, domestic violence and institutional abuse against disabled people. Named 'Stay Safe', the project is one of very few based in a disabled people's organisation (DPO) to tackle domestic and sexual violence as well as hate crime, bullying and harassment of disabled people.[17]

The project has three aims:

- To provide one-to-one advocacy and support to disabled people experiencing hate crime and domestic violence.

- To inform disabled people of their rights and encourage them to speak out about violence.

- To capacity-build local agencies to provide an inclusive service to all, and change local policy and practice.

A year into the project, over half of Stay Safe's casework is around domestic and sexual violence – the overwhelming majority of victims of domestic violence seen by Stay Safe are women, from a range of local communities and backgrounds, from their early twenties to their seventies. Many had been in contact with other agencies, or have been referred through the local multi-agency risk assessment conference (MARAC), of which Stay Safe is an active member. Others, particularly Deaf women, had not been able to contact local agencies because they were not accessible to them. Because Disability Action staff have specialist skills and knowledge around independent living and supporting disabled people, the project is able to provide a holistic service, for example assisting disabled clients to access a social care package, get help with travel, or obtain specialist equipment.

The key aim of the project is to develop good practice that can be of use beyond the local arena. Stay Safe is working with local domestic violence agencies, the police, housing providers and others to change the way that disabled people are dealt with if they are victims of hate crime or domestic violence. At the time of writing, the project is negotiating to provide training to the local police, and has had small successes in raising issues and changing the way that some agencies deal with disabled clients. It has also been raising issues at national level, such as the discrimination experienced by Deaf women seeking a refuge space.[18]

The work done by organisations in Leeds, Glasgow and Waltham Forest shows the value of collaborative working between disabled women and domestic violence agencies. However, these local examples will only lead to lasting change if national strategies are in place, and if all local partnerships effectively involve disabled women.

Principles of good practice

Since the early 1980s there has been excellent work around domestic violence and wider issues of violence against women and girls. There are generic projects, and there are projects supporting women from a range of diverse communities whose needs are not always met by generic services. 'Mainstream' services are expected to be inclusive, from refuges to independent domestic violence advisers, the police and the courts. Many of these projects are dealing with some disabled women but, as the Women's Aid research shows, there is still a long way to go.

Throughout this book, a major conclusion has been, as discussed in the next chapter, that a sea change in current practice is essential in order for disabled women to get the services they deserve, and to get justice. In our view, good practice in reducing domestic violence must flow from some key principles:

- A social model approach that seeks to remove barriers for disabled women.

- An inclusive approach to all forms of violence against women.

- Nothing about us without us: partnerships with disabled women at all levels.

The social model of disability: removing barriers

A social model approach, first of all, means removing barriers at all stages and taking an inclusive approach to the accessibility and usability of processes and services from the outset – disabled women as equals, not 'add-ons' to services. The next two chapters cover the practical issues that must be addressed by all agencies if disabled women are to get support and justice on an equal basis to non-disabled women.

Women With Disabilities Australia (1999) identified an accessible service as one that is:

- easy to find out about
- easily understood
- easy to get to
- easy to use.

They argue that a service such as a refuge is accessible when the woman who wants to use it:

- feels welcome
- knows she will get the right assistance when she needs it
- is confident she will get what she wants, when she needs it.

Below we set out some key components which we believe are needed to ensure that disabled women are safe. Our overall suggestions, based on our experiences as activists and practitioners, complement the research recommendations outlined in the next two chapters.

PREVENTION

- At a local level, organisations reaching out to disabled women and girls – in the communities where they live, in residential homes, in sheltered housing, in day centres, in mainstream and special schools and in youth clubs – and doing this in a way that is accessible and relevant, and that informs them of their rights. We would ask: how much of your material features disabled women? Can we recognise our experience?

- Most of all, an inclusive approach to independent living that does not leave disabled women dependent on the goodwill of those who would control our lives.

- Challenging assumptions – of service providers and wider society, and of non-disabled people, that disabled men are not perpetrators, that disabled women are not perpetrators, that disabled women are not sexually abused, etc.

- Raising awareness amongst disabled women of what domestic violence is and where to get help. Not only voluntary sector organisations, but police Safer Neighbourhood teams are a key factor both in prevention and in encouraging disabled women (and men) to report all forms of domestic violence, hate crime and abuse. They have the potential to make links with disabled individuals, by for example speaking to people in their neighbourhoods and to users as well as staff in day centres and group homes. Telling disabled women about successful actions and prosecutions – that things are changing, so it is worth going to the police.

INFORMATION

- Domestic violence information that is inclusive, relevant to disabled women, reaches us where we live, work and study, and is accessible. A good example are the posters developed by Women's Aid that are targeted specifically at disabled women, but we would like to see generic publicity that is inclusive.

- Information about access to services. If services are inclusive and this is made clear, then disabled women are more likely to approach them. Otherwise we will assume that these services are 'not for us'.

REPORTING AND GETTING HELP

- Accessible places for disabled women to report domestic violence and to get help. This includes access for Deaf women via SMS text and face-to-face using an interpreter. It is essential that disabled women can trust that they will be listened to.

SAFE AND APPROPRIATE OPTIONS FOR REFUGE
THAT MEET A RANGE OF NEEDS

- As refuge services are cut back, it is all the more essential that those that remain are inclusive, as well as specialist services being maintained and developed. This is not only about physical access (wheelchair access, means of warning Deaf women of an emergency, etc.) but about what type of services are available, for example 24-hour staffing or staff who have been trained to communicate with women with learning difficulties. It is also about challenging bullying towards disabled women in refuges.

- Where a refuge space is not the best option, other options such as the Sanctuary scheme can help keep the woman safe, but must be appropriate and accessible and not make her situation worse.

- Institutional care is *not* an appropriate option for women experiencing domestic or sexual violence.

HOLISTIC SUPPORT FOR VICTIMS THAT IS APPROPRIATE AND TAILORED TO OUR NEEDS

- Advocacy services that understand the social care system, the Deaf community or the disabled community, or have links with organisations that do. Partnership working between domestic violence and disability advocates is an excellent way to address this.

HOLISTIC SUPPORT: GOOD PRACTICE

Beverley Lewis House, the East London safe house for women with learning difficulties, which we discussed earlier in this chapter, is staffed 24 hours per day because women with learning difficulties need immediate access to someone to talk with. Staff are on duty all night because they have found that women who needed to talk during the night are unable to hold back until the morning staff arrive. The refuge also provides independent living training and support so that women who have previously been 'looked after' can move on. This of course is similar to the practice of some domestic violence support organisations, in particular those that work with minority communities, to support women whose lives were controlled and have never developed the skills to live independently. For those organisations, it is only a short step to including disabled women.

Those few disabled people's organisations which are providing independent domestic violence advocacy are able to provide a comprehensive service because they have the knowledge and understanding of, for example, social care support options or available equipment or adaptations, so that a disabled woman who was previously dependent for her care on an abusive partner can live independently. Domestic violence agencies that currently do not have such specialist knowledge can gain this by working in partnership with disabled people's organisations.

JUSTICE FOR DISABLED WOMEN[19]

- Any investigation by the police must treat the woman as a reliable witness, not a 'vulnerable adult' and keep her at the centre of the process. This means, most crucially, trained police officers who understand disability equality, are good communicators and who will get advice if they need it, and who have access to the means to meet a woman's access needs.

- Effective prosecution of the perpetrators of violence against disabled women involves ensuring that the woman herself as a witness is properly supported, by use of appropriate intermediaries[20] and special measures. The use of intermediaries and special measures has helped obtain convictions, for example in recent rape cases involving people with learning difficulties. The Crown Prosecution Service has also issued guidance to its own prosecutors so that disabled people get justice, and are not, for example, treated as 'unreliable witnesses' or assumptions made about their capacity.

SHORT-TERM AND LONG-TERM RECOVERY

- Counselling services are needed that are appropriate and accessible to disabled women, are social model based, and where possible involve peer support.

- Most crucially, the social care system needs to be flexible enough to provide short-term support while a woman recovers from the violence and learns new independent living skills.

LEARNING AND TRAINING

Some of this good practice is already happening in places, as practitioners become more aware of disabled women's issues. Through training[21] and learning, case reviews and equality impact assessments conducted by local multi-agency forums, these isolated examples of good practice can become commonplace. It is not difficult to include the experiences of disabled women in existing CAADA and other training. At a time when resources are limited, sharing of skills between domestic violence organisations and disabled people's organisations can also help improve practice. Above all, these practical measures must be underpinned by national and local strategies that include the reality of the lives of disabled women, and address attitudes and assumptions about disabled women.

An inclusive approach to violence against women

A SINGLE APPROACH TO DOMESTIC VIOLENCE AGAINST ALL WOMEN

As we have argued earlier in this chapter, an approach to violence against disabled women separate from that adopted to violence against non-disabled women leads to unequal, disempowering practices. We would argue that a single approach is possible, and that the current model used for domestic violence, with some changes, is the best model to use. The key benefits of this approach are:

- Joint working by a range of agencies so that support is coordinated and knowledge and expertise is shared.

- The involvement of grassroots agencies who know the victim, understand her personal situation, her cultural background and her wishes.

- A focus on keeping the victim safe.

- A framework for risk assessment and minimising risk that also accepts that the woman herself has choices to make.

- The possibility of challenge by those local agencies if statutory agencies are not fulfilling their duties.

- An externally monitored process that is reasonably transparent.

We can see no reason why this model should not be used for all violence against women. A single approach does not of course mean a uniform approach – different women require different forms of support, and responses must be tailored to diverse needs.

A WIDER DEFINITION OF DOMESTIC VIOLENCE

As set out earlier in this chapter, we would strongly argue that the current definitions of domestic violence need to be rewritten to reflect the specific reality of disabled women's lives. A new definition of domestic violence would include:

> Any form of abuse, physical, psychological, financial, sexual or otherwise that happens in a domestic or intimate setting and is perpetrated by partners, family members, paid or unpaid carers, and others who have close contact with the victim.

A specific protocol could be added to domestic violence procedures for dealing with abusers who are paid or are volunteers and are using their position to abuse disabled people and others.

SITUATIONAL NOT INDIVIDUAL VULNERABILITY

To tackle all forms of violence against disabled women and men, it is essential that we move away from the idea of there being groups or individuals who are in themselves vulnerable to one of situational vulnerability, as set out earlier in this chapter.

REVISING RISK ASSESSMENT PROCEDURES TO
INCLUDE DISABLED WOMEN'S LIVES

This in effect is the model adopted by CAADA in its risk assessment procedure, which focuses on the situation of a woman experiencing domestic violence and any heightened risk that might arise from it, such as repeat incidents or the risk of 'honour-based violence'.

We would argue that the current risk framework used in domestic violence should be used for all violence against disabled people but that it needs to be widened to include the specific risks faced by disabled women. Clearly, for disabled women as for non-disabled women in a domestic violence situation, factors such as social isolation, pregnancy, child contact, repeat victimisation or sexual assault are likely to heighten the risks. In addition to these risks identified in the CAADA framework (CAADA 2011), we would argue for a model that assesses the *unique risks* faced by a disabled woman if:

- she is socially isolated and has no contact outside her immediate family and/or paid carers, or if she is living in residential care, outside her paid carers and other professionals

- she is dependent on relatives or a partner for all or most of her care or support needs or to get out and about

- she depends on family or partner to speak for her, for example if they interpret for her or communicate on her behalf

- she rarely or never goes out of the home

- the threat of institutionalisation is being used against her (including of sectioning under the Mental Health Act)

- the abuser is controlling her medication or disability equipment.

This model focuses on situational vulnerability rather than vulnerability because the woman has an impairment – in most cases, impairment is not *per se* a determinant of risk. Disabled women are of course not exempt from risk factors such as a perpetrator using their pregnancy as a means of control, 'honour-based violence' or forced marriage.[22]

If you can't get through the door, you can't have the conversation: working in partnership with disabled women and disabled people's organisations

None of the changes we have outlined can happen without a partnership with disabled people and in particular with disabled women, at all levels, in policy and in practice.

In the disabled people's movement, we talk about 'Nothing about us without us', as discussed throughout this book. This operates on an individual level where whatever the level of impairment, a disabled woman's wishes must be respected, she must be listened to and supported to make her own decisions. It also operates at a strategic level where disabled women must be involved in formulating policies, strategies and protocols around domestic violence. In our experience this needs to involve more than a 'token' disabled woman, as the experience can be very alienating otherwise. While professionals who 'know about disability' have a part to play, their perspectives are not necessarily those of disabled people.

The current political climate is one where involvement is seen as less important, but domestic violence policy-makers and practitioners cannot afford to exclude disabled women. The movement against violence against women has a long history of empowering survivors to be change-makers. As two disabled women who have spent many years trying to get these issues on the agenda, we know that involvement cannot happen just by asking disabled women to attend established forums, working groups, etc., on other people's terms. Those processes need to be made accessible and relevant to us – whether by not using jargon that outsiders may not understand, or by ensuring that minutes or venues are accessible. As the Glasgow example shows, disabled women have a lot to say about domestic violence – on a personal as well as on a strategic level. Because we have been excluded for so long, some disabled women may need time and capacity building to develop skills at working at a strategic level.

Key areas of involvement are:

- Board membership of domestic violence services, whether refuges or other services.

- Local strategic safety partnerships, particularly domestic violence boards.

- National strategic boards on domestic violence.

- Police and Crown Prosecution Service independent advisory groups.

- Serious case reviews where the victim is a disabled woman.

Disabled women and disability organisations should also be involved in equality impact assessment and audits at local level to establish what the gaps are in practice and approach around disabled women. This is not just about consultation but partnership, and should include disabled women with the necessary expertise.

As we have said throughout our two chapters, and as the research has shown, disabled people's organisations (DPOs) are key players in any approaches to domestic violence. In spite of threats to their survival in the current political and economic climate, more DPOs are becoming involved in local community safety partnerships, primarily around hate crime. Encouraging involvement of DPOs in domestic violence boards would be a positive step in ensuring that disability expertise is available at local level. At national level, organisations such as the UK Disabled People's Council, which has been working on violence against disabled people for many years, have a crucial role to play in shaping policies and practices that benefit disabled women.

In conclusion: a strategic approach

So far, change has been about individual disabled women, with a few organisations and their allies, trying to raise the issues and influence policy. It has been, by and large, about pockets of good practice. There has been no strategic approach to domestic violence and disabled women and, significantly, very little effective involvement and empowerment of disabled women.

At a time in the UK when services are being cut, when disabled people and women's rights are being pushed off the agenda, and many women's organisations are at risk of closure, some would argue that looking at changing the way we do things so that disabled women are included is a luxury that domestic violence services cannot afford. But it is precisely in these difficult times that organisations need to look at how they can most effectively reach and support those most at risk, and challenge the very discrimination which creates those risks.

Action has started to happen by some national and local bodies around disability hate crime, at least at a strategic level, and some engagement has taken place with disabled people and their organisations. A similar process must happen around domestic violence.

Notes

1   But many other European countries have been late in endorsing an independent living model – in France, for example, a high proportion of young people with physical impairments still live in group homes; in Greece and the countries which were formerly part of the Eastern bloc, oppressive institutions are only slowly (and often reluctantly) being transformed into more benign 'group homes'.

2   Nevertheless, in most areas of the UK, up to half of children with statements are still educated in special schools.

3   Twenty-two per cent of respondents to a 2011 Ipsos MORI survey for Mencap said they would be bothered a little/rather a lot/a great deal if someone in their family married a person with a learning difficulty, and only 23 per cent if someone with a learning difficulty had children. This is a marked improvement on earlier surveys of attitudes towards disabled people, in spite of the rising numbers of reports of hostility against disabled people, and against people with learning difficulties in particular (Mencap 2011).

4   Frances Inglis murdered her adult son Thomas by injecting him with heroin after he sustained a brain injury, because she wanted to 'free him from a "living hell" of permanent disability, disfigurement and round-the-clock care.' She was given nine years for murder and lost her appeal, but had the support of her family who described her as a 'devoted mother' who carried out a 'loving and courageous act'. The family has called for a review of the way that severely disabled people's lives can be legally ended (*Daily Mail* 2010).

5   Brent Martin was a young man with learning difficulties. In August 2007 he was viciously attacked and murdered for a five pound bet. Before his death his three attackers partially stripped him, chased him through the streets and subjected him to a sustained attack in four different locations.

6   'Muppet' is sometimes used as an offensive term for a person with learning difficulties, and rarely challenged. In recent episodes of *Emmerdale* and *EastEnders*, characters were heard to call each other 'muppet' as a term of endearment.

7   Section 146 of the Criminal Justice Act 2003.

8   The report was based on a scrutiny of media reports across the UK. Police force records are incomplete, particularly where hate crime against disabled people is concerned – until 2009, police forces did not record disability hate crime. Other research by MIND and the Equality and Human Rights Commission focusing on specific impairment groups showed similar patterns.

9   In research in Glasgow by Wise Women for the Daisie Project (2010), 73 per cent of the disabled women surveyed had experienced domestic abuse.

10   This was in fact the response to the questioner at the event from the speaker from Ashiana, a project for young women from South Asian backgrounds who have experienced domestic or sexual violence.

11   In this model, Planet A is domestic violence and the surrounding ideological assumptions, Planet B child protection and welfare, and Planet C visitation and contact.

12   Mainly via the MARAC multi-agency risk assessment conference forums which exist in all localities, and are subject to a national scrutiny process.

13   In 2010, new guidance allowed the victim to be present at Safeguarding meetings. In practice, unless the disabled person has an independent advocate to support them, he or she is unlikely to be meaningfully involved in these formal and often inaccessible processes.

14   As evidenced by the deaths of David Askew in Manchester, Fiona Pilkington and Francesca Hardwick in Leicester, and many others.

15   Information for Deaf women about Violence Against Women. © Deaf Women Against Violence/Wise Women (see Deaf Women Against Violence/Wise Women 2011).

16   Ruth Bashall is chair of Disability Action Waltham Forest and was instrumental in setting up the project.

17 The only other DPO project we are aware of that covers both hate crime and domestic violence is an advocacy project run by South London-based Greenwich Association of Disabled People (see www.gad.org.uk).

18 The project was informed by several refuges they could not accept Deaf women 'for health and safety reasons', yet off-the-peg systems are available at relatively low cost which provide a vibrating pager to warn Deaf residents of an emergency. This is a requirement of the Equality Act.

19 Satisfaction rates and confidence in the police amongst disabled people are lower than those amongst non-disabled people (Flatley *et al.* 2010). The London Public Attitude Survey (Goode and Ellis 2008) identified a 10 per cent gap in satisfaction levels regarding the service received, between disabled and non-disabled victims of violent crime. There are no specific statistics for disabled women. The lack of confidence is reflected in how the police deal with serious crimes against disabled people: for example there is a 7 per cent lower sanction detection rate in cases involving disabled victims of domestic violence than in those involving a non-disabled victim. Appropriate risk management measures were less likely to have been taken, and there was a very large (43%) difference in whether appropriate steps had been taken in relation to children living in the house.

20 Intermediaries are independent professionals, not advocates, and are there to give advice to police and the CPS to help achieve more productive interviews and at court to get best evidence at trial. They can facilitate the communication process in court, advise on how a witness communicates and their levels of understanding, and how it would be best to question them to get best evidence. It is essential that intermediaries understand the needs of disabled people, and treat them with respect and as equals.

21 Currently, for example, the generic training for the police around domestic and sexual violence includes very little about disability equality from a social model perspective. It is focused on a vulnerable adult model which may get in the way of dealing effectively with abuse against disabled people.

22 In response to research by Voice UK and Respond, the Home Office has produced guidance on tackling forced marriage against people with learning difficulties. The research showed that women and men with learning difficulties from South Asian and other communities were at high risk of forced marriage by families, who saw marriage as a means of providing a carer and continuing support, or of facilitating the entry into the UK for the spouse, or even of 'curing' the disabled person – yet forced marriage is violence in itself, and leads to domestic violence, sexual assault and rape and loss of human rights (Foreign and Commonwealth Office 2010).

Chapter 7

Ideas for Moving Forward

Good Practice and Recommendations

Building on the previous chapters by Brenda Ellis and Ruth Bashall, this chapter is about good practice for agencies working with disabled women who have experienced domestic violence and abuse. As we have mentioned throughout this book, the existing literature suggests that disabled women experience significantly more abuse than non-disabled women, so it is all the more important for agencies to respond effectively. In addition, an important finding from this study is that all the women interviewed believed that being disabled made the abuse worse and limited their capacity to get away or to take other preventive measures. Perpetrators often used a woman's impairment as part of the abuse, increasing both the abuser's power and control over her, and her vulnerability and isolation. Yet, when also caring for the woman, perpetrators were frequently seen by others as being self-sacrificing and beyond reproach. Women who had no recourse to public funds, and whose first language was not English, were particularly trapped as, even when they had attempted to leave, without access to support or funding they often could not access the services they needed and might not have the command of English required to try to get their needs met. There were also intersecting issues for BMER women, lesbian women and women abused by their paid carers.

Thus, disabled women experience a greater need for support services and require sensitive and appropriate responses from those that do exist. However, as our surveys demonstrate, the opposite is often the case, with greater need being accompanied by far less provision. Abused disabled women therefore often lose out in all respects, as we have emphasised throughout this book.

Our recommendations for good practice grew out of the problems and discontent that we identified among abused disabled women seeking services and help. The main agencies disabled women contacted for help in our study included the police, social services/adult services, refuges and domestic violence services, outreach projects, disability organisations and housing agencies. Statutory agencies in particular, as discussed in Chapter 4, failed to provide a helpful response to disabled women. This outcome is a signal that change is needed. It is worth reiterating the significant point from our previous discussions that, when asked which organisations had been most helpful, with the odd exception of a particular individual worker, refuge or disabled people's organisation, almost all the interviewees could not identify any agency at all. Not one.

There are some ways forward, though. Against this general backdrop of unsatisfactory responses, our research identified the following ideas, both about needs that should be met, in terms of services for disabled women experiencing domestic violence and abuse, and about social action and change in order to do so.

A 'step-change' is needed

It was clear throughout the research, from the sort of service experiences noted above and from the surveys reported in the previous chapters, that what is needed is better services and better partnership between the service-providing sectors involved. There is the need for a 'sea change' or a 'step-change' in how both domestic violence and disability services respond to disabled women experiencing abuse, and for a general cultural change in agency attitudes. Our study found, as noted in Chapter 4, that a major change of this type is necessary at an operational level in terms of how the helping services respond. But it is also needed at a strategic management level to make the issue a core one for relevant agencies, so that it is taken seriously. Once the abuse of disabled women is seen as a core issue, it can be included in all relevant work plans, grant applications and budgets, and can then be prioritised at an appropriate level by both agency management and staff.

It was clear from the research that many agencies and individual workers have the best of intentions. However, it appears that the needs of abused disabled women are very far indeed from being viewed as a central concern, alongside other similar core issues in domestic violence work, even in services specifically meant to provide assistance. This was even more the case for many disability and disabled people's organisations. In our study, good practice was extremely patchy within both the disability and the domestic violence sectors, which still work largely in isolation from each other.

What needs to be improved for making practice better

The underlying issue that needs to be addressed, as identified by organisations in our surveys in both the domestic violence and the disability sectors, was the lack of staff and money to enable them to take on disabled women's needs. This situation will quite probably be aggravated by present and future cutbacks in public services. However, a whole raft of recommendations and ideas for good practice emerged from our study and from abused disabled women's advice that could assist in rectifying these gaps and shortcomings in provision. In attempting to collate this huge range of possibilities, some resounding themes stand out, drawing on the above discussion of good practice needs, and on the detailed considerations in the previous two chapters on activism and policy. We discuss these general recommendations in this section. Later in the chapter, we provide a list of the wider range of recommendations we identified, classified into bullet-pointed sections, for ease of use by professionals working on the issue and seeking a quick reference point for anchoring their work on disability and domestic violence and abuse.

The first major theme is clearly the need for more comprehensive services for disabled women experiencing domestic violence across the board and in all sectors. Currently, as we have emphasised throughout, services for disabled women experiencing domestic violence are often overlooked, neglected, inadequate or non-existent, with the effect that women in these situations may feel completely abandoned.

The second overall theme is the need for more training and awareness-raising for professionals and agencies in all relevant sectors, including the police, health and adult social services, as well as specialist domestic violence and disability projects. Disability equality and domestic violence training of this type might be expected to include demythologising both disability and domestic violence, challenging prevailing attitudes, and overcoming fear, anxiety and lack of commitment among service providers. Good practice in this area suggests that the equality training offered needs to use both the social model of disability and gendered understandings of domestic violence and abuse, to be culturally sensitive, to be aware of issues of diversity and difference, and, if possible, to be delivered by disabled women themselves, with expertise in the area.

For both of these major issues, the provision of services and of improved training, nothing can move forward without resource allocation, supported by policy direction. Our major recommendations are therefore that taking the issue seriously means providing at least some resources, and the development both of commitment and also of direct championing (even in minor ways) for the cause. Otherwise, little will change. Our hope has been that the findings of this study would both shock and push local authorities and the government into action. At the time of writing, however, this possibility may be compromised by the cutbacks in public expenditure announced in 2010 and expected to dominate subsequent years. Thus, services are likely to get worse rather than better, with severe cuts being made in individual service provision by local authorities struggling to deal with hugely decreased public funding in the future.

Overall recommendations for domestic violence services and for disability organisations

For domestic violence organisations, the improvements needed would be expected to include continuing to increase the accessibility of premises, building on the work Women's Aid has already conducted in this area, to make sure that all refuges, outreach and other domestic violence services are fully accessible. Good practice would also include developing clear and full disability policies to guide the organisation's work, and collecting improved data on disabled women using the service. Of key importance is the provision of increased, high quality disability equality training in domestic violence organisations, specially designed for this purpose. Training of this type would be expected to differ from general disability and domestic violence training in that it could be assumed that the workers would already have a considerable knowledge of domestic abuse. While such training exists, and an aim of Women's Aid is to improve it, we found, as we have discussed earlier, that it is often inadequate for the task, and this sometimes shows in the attitudes and lack of knowledge of staff. Women's Aid and other domestic violence organisations are of course the key service-providers for women experiencing domestic abuse. Thus, while domestic violence training would be helpful for all professionals and volunteers working with disabled women, disability equality and domestic violence training could be viewed as essential for the specialist domestic violence organisations themselves, which provide vital direct and often emergency services.

Any improvements in domestic violence organisations and in their accessibility, together with professional disability equality training, need also to be publicised so disabled women are aware of them. If disabled women do not know what domestic abuse services are available, improved resources are of little help. Good local practice of this type can be assisted by the national organisations in the field. In fact, specific attempts to reach, involve and provide for disabled women experiencing domestic violence need to be embedded, in a systematic way, in both the management and the operation of Women's Aid and other domestic violence services nationally, as well as locally. Unless the issue is championed at the national level, the spreading of good practice and of service improvement is unlikely.

Disabled people's organisations with a relevant brief need also to take on the issue of domestic violence as both a management and an operational concern, as previously noted, rather than tending to regard it as 'not their issue' as is often the case at present. A useful starting point would be for relevant disability organisations to monitor and keep data on domestic violence and abuse. Leading on from this, there is a need to build joint work with domestic violence services, and to develop effective referral processes and pathways, recognising the specific needs that some disabled women may have. Overall, the most important recommendation is for disabled people's and disability organisations to provide appropriate practical service responses, in tandem with Women's Aid and other local domestic violence specialists, including providing informed support. This is likely to mean the development, also, of agency policies on domestic violence and abuse for disability organisations. Good practice would include providing domestic violence and abuse training for disability workers, as discussed above, as well as developing focused advocacy and a general awareness about the issue as something that disabled women might ask for help with.

For both domestic violence and disability organisations, it would be best practice to employ staff with relevant expertise, or even to work towards having a dedicated worker in the team specialising in disability and domestic violence. Such a worker could then assist in developing services and policy, and provide support to disabled abuse survivors. They would need to be women, where possible, even in those disabled people's organisations that currently only have male staff. (Domestic violence organisations, on the other hand, are usually staffed by women.)

The involvement of disabled women in service provision

Following the principle of 'Nothing about us without us', one of the most significant findings that resonated throughout our study was the ongoing need for interaction between disabled and non-disabled women, both as service providers and service users. The research data and the reflections in the previous two chapters suggest that in terms, for example, of the provision of domestic violence and disability equality training and public awareness-raising, the best approach is for such education and training to be provided by disabled women expert in domestic violence issues.

The involvement of disabled women in service development is of key importance at all levels, but particularly for management, so that disabled women representatives are able to contribute to decision-making and have some power in the organisations concerned. Thus, involving disabled women at both strategic and operational levels in the work and the management of relevant agencies was seen to be key, enabling them to develop improved policies, strategic and policy reviews, service plans and service monitoring, directly informed by disabled women themselves.

Disabled women's views and direct advice

Abused disabled women interviewed in the study believed strongly that the issue of disabled women's experience of domestic violence should be mainstreamed and have greater visibility among all relevant organisations, so that services are sensitised and able to respond more effectively. Abused disabled women to whom we talked made the following specific suggestions for good practice by agencies:

- Be informed about disabled women's needs.

- Take advice from, and consult with, disabled women.

- Develop accessible services.

- Provide accessible well-publicised domestic violence services (including refuge accommodation) that disabled women know about.

- Do not threaten disabled women with institutionalisation if no refuge space is available.

- Develop good accessible alternative accommodation, both temporary and permanent, plus support to use it.

- Develop disability equality schemes and reviews with input from disabled women.

- Take disabled women seriously and avoid being patronising.

The disabled women with whom we spoke were clear that policies and services cannot be developed independently of disabled women's views and expertise, as discussed above. The need for professionals in all services to be more aware of the issue, and pick up on it, was also highlighted, as was the need to develop greater sensitivity in asking disabled women about their situations and enabling them to disclose any abuse. For women from black and minority ethnic communities, the importance was emphasised of support services that are run and led by people of similar backgrounds and who are sensitised to issues of disability and domestic violence. Safety was identified as the priority issue, but was talked about in terms not only of physical safety but of emotional and cultural safety, and a feeling of being secure which might include having access to specific foods, religious practices and hygiene expectations.

Disabled women had a variety of further suggestions for improved services including, first and foremost, more accessible refuge services to assist disabled women escaping violence, and support to get there. Other recommendations included a telephone helpline run specifically for disabled women affected by domestic violence and abuse (even if this is only possible for limited periods of time), as well as on-line counsellors or advisers who specialise in domestic abuse and disability. Along these lines, the provision of more information to disabled women about specialist organisations and other services would be of help. Our interviewees highlighted the issue of being able to take care packages and PAs with them when going into an accessible refuge. The latter was identified as a crucial issue, as we discuss in more detail below. Without it, a disabled woman's options may be severely limited.

Our interviewees also stressed that attention should be given to where disabled women are permanently or temporarily re-housed, in terms of ease of use of both the accommodation and the wider area. Accessible accommodation needs to be safe in itself, and to be in areas that are safe for disabled women to use. Further, in terms of housing, consideration should also be given to providing tenancy agreements for accessible accommodation in the sole name of the disabled person, so that it might be easier to evict an abusive partner.

As discussed in several earlier chapters, we identified the issue of abuse by PAs or paid carers. Our interviewees suggested the establishment of an external agency that could provide supervision and support to staff and to disabled women employing assistants or carers, and the creation of a 'buddy' system for those employing PAs and paid carers to share expertise and support.

Specific advice for disability and domestic violence organisations

Disabled women's specific advice to disabled people's and disability organisations included training staff on domestic violence awareness, but went far beyond this. It also included mentioning domestic violence in general agency publicity; putting out more public information about domestic abuse (to be available in a variety of venues and formats); discussing issues of abuse openly within the disability organisation; self-confidence courses for women; and supporting abuse survivors in recognising and naming what is happening to them, and being able to formulate ways to tell someone.

In regard to domestic violence organisations, our informants advised that, as well as the urgent need for more accessible refuge places and the other general issues noted above, domestic violence services need to continue to use appropriate publicity, leaflets and other information to reach disabled women in a variety of formats, and to improve accessible accommodation in small ways as well as large (the provision of small, portable disability aids could make all the difference for some women, for example). Also advised was work to develop greater awareness around the issues of disability and domestic violence for non-disabled women using services, as well as staff. This might help to counteract the embarrassment, ignorance and even slight panic that both non-disabled refuge workers and residents might experience when a disabled woman arrives, needing refuge.

The statutory sector and community care packages

The statutory sector has a key role to play in providing support to disabled women experiencing domestic violence and abuse. Recommendations for the sector include the adoption of adequate definitions of domestic violence that take account of the range of needs and experiences of abused disabled women, the development of better methods of recording and monitoring, and the provision of services, guidance, professional training and public education. Overall, attention to the needs of disabled women who have experienced domestic abuse should be 'mainstreamed' in the statutory sector, written into work targets and integrated into all relevant budgets, work plans and policies. At the moment, it is often tacked on or overlooked until a disabled woman needs help.

It is important to note that the governmental national guidance, *No Secrets* (Department of Health and Home Office 2005), on meeting the needs of adults at risk could, for some situations, be sensitively adapted by local authorities specifically to assist disabled women experiencing domestic violence. This is further discussed in the next chapter, and was also specifically alluded to in terms of very often actual unhelpfulness – rather than helpfulness – in Chapter 5. However, as was discussed, the 'vulnerable adults' framework may not be the right one in which to provide services for disabled women who have been exposed to violence. Separate support services are likely to be more appropriate.

Disabled women often live in premises that have been adapted for them and where they have a care package of organised services to support them. If they then have to leave home due to domestic abuse, this situation can present an almost insurmountable problem. Thus, if such a care package could be made portable and it was possible to transfer it to a new local authority area fairly easily, this would be of enormous help. Some local authorities have reciprocal agreements along these lines. Such transferable provision sometimes includes disabled women being able to retain their own personal assistants and carers (where the carer agrees to this outcome), including when going into a refuge.

As an example of good practice, the Leeds City Council Domestic Violence Team (formerly the Leeds Inter-Agency Project) has worked in partnership with Leeds City Council Adult Social Care services to produce guidelines of this type on community care packages in cases of domestic violence. One of their managers whom we talked with explained that:

> The guidance means that adult services are able to respond effectively to women experiencing domestic violence and that any community care package they may have does not have to come to an end because they move house. Reassessments are conducted to see what changes are required but the package continues. We believe that making community care packages portable in this way would greatly assist disabled women in other local authorities.

This helpful guidance may not be able to continue under the new funding regimes and cutbacks but remain as a beacon of good practice. In our study, we learned from both our interviews with disabled women and with agencies that the fact that they would lose their package if they left home due to violence worked to prevent them doing so, even if they had been extremely severely abused, possibly over a long period. It was not possible for them to take such a risk. The further development of policies to avoid this outcome would, therefore, be not only helpful but potentially life-changing – or life-saving.

Detailed recommendations for good practice

This section is designed for ease of practical use by busy practitioners and policy-makers. We present in much more detail here the specific recommendations that emerged from our study and that we have outlined above, laying them out in sections and using a bullet-point format for easy visibility.

The provision of services

- The wide range of support services needed should include more accessible refuge accommodation, together with accessible outreach, advocacy and other support services.

- Also needed are floating support workers to support abused disabled women who wish to stay in their own homes.

- Accessibility of services needs to be thought about in broad terms (see below), and not be limited to, for example, the needs of wheelchair users.

- Disabled women may need to be able to take their care package with them if they move due to domestic violence, or to negotiate a new one in the new area.

- There can be, in some situations, a need for higher levels of focused support than provided for non-disabled women, and greater advocacy, telephone contact and outreach to sort out difficulties before a disabled woman might be ready or able to leave home for alternative accommodation (for example, a refuge).

- Support and protocols continue to be needed to make the personalisation agenda and the self-directed support programme effective for abused disabled women.

- Partnership working arrangements need to be developed to ensure that disability and domestic violence organisations work together to meet the needs of abused disabled women.

Disability and domestic violence policies, training and public education

- Domestic violence and disability equality training needs to be implemented across all sectors, and there is a need for public education on the issue.

- Such training and public education should be provided, where possible, by disabled women expert in domestic violence issues.

- It must be based on the social model of disability, a gendered understanding of domestic violence and abuse, and the overcoming of fear, anxiety and apparent lack of commitment among service providers.

- Training and awareness-raising for the general public need also to address lack of knowledge, and to challenge negative stereotypes and prevailing social attitudes about abused disabled women.

- Both professional training and public education programmes would be expected to include material on 'disability oppression' as caused by social barriers (while acknowledging that individual impairments can lead to particular difficulties).

- They would also be expected to include diversity issues, specific for example to disabled BMER women, lesbians, and other minorities, as well as to both older and young disabled women. Further, such training programmes should note the impacts of such issues as social class, poverty and immigration.

- Also required would be British Sign Language interpreters where possible, and the meeting of other access needs, using accessible formats and venues.

- Training could be delivered in phases where necessary, to raise its profile.

Disabled women with knowledge of domestic violence should be involved in all developments in policy and practice

- Funding may be able to be sought for dedicated posts: for example, a disability worker in domestic violence organisations or a domestic violence specialist in the major disability organisations. Ideally, mainstreamed funding needs to be aimed for, to embed this provision and make it sustainable.

- Disabled women with knowledge about the issue need to be consulted about all developments in policy and practice and invited to participate in strategy development, service planning, decision-making meetings and advisory groups, preferably with payment or at least compensation.

- The involvement of disabled women needs to be monitored, including in take-up of services and participation in service development.

- Management roles in the relevant agencies need to be consciously made available to disabled women.

All relevant agencies need to aim to provide accessible premises and services

- All relevant agencies could usefully take advice on providing for the needs of abused disabled women and accessibility.

- A variety of different formats needs to be utilised in order to provide accessible publicity and information.

- Complex needs that disabled women may have, depending on their individual impairments and which may extend beyond physical accessibility, need to be catered for.

- The provision of fully accessible adapted accommodation for disabled women seeking refuge is vital, such as:

  ° for women with mobility difficulties, a few examples: lifts, ramps, bathroom and kitchen adaptations and even floor surfaces

  ° for women from the Deaf community, a few examples: BSL provision, email, flashing-light fire alarms and vibrating pillows (for night-time fire alarms), and text phones including, importantly, for helplines

  ° for women with visual impairments, a few examples: appropriate new technology where possible, large print information and colour-contrasted environments.

- Further small adaptations such as handrails, desk loops, personal listeners, kettle pourers, accessible IT, small moveable aids and extra lights (which are fairly inexpensive) can be relatively easily provided.

Measures to reach out to abused disabled women about domestic violence

As an overarching principle, these measures should emphasise taking disabled women seriously and avoid patronising responses:

- Measures could be expected to include the provision of more publicity, posters and leaflets about the issue, together with more information for service providers, and for disabled women themselves.

- Agencies need to work directly with disabled women wherever possible to raise awareness of domestic violence, and to spread information about available services and where to get help. This may on occasion include safety planning for individual disabled women who have experienced abuse.

- Steps could usefully be taken to reach out to disabled women who are very isolated and not able to access any services, for example through new use of local radio, information in accessible toilets for disabled people, and so on.

- In order to 'get it right', relevant agencies need as a principle to involve disabled women (both service users and workers) in decision-making about what is required to improve services and to raise awareness, and what would work best.

Further detailed recommendations for domestic violence organisations

- Building on good practice where it already exists, local domestic violence organisations need to become fully inclusive for all women, including disabled women.

- There is an urgent need for more facilities of all types for disabled women, embedded across all domestic violence services (including outreach, advocacy and refuge) and for the comprehensive provision of high quality disability equality and domestic violence training.

- Domestic violence services could usefully develop specific disability policies.

- All refuge organisations need to develop full physical access, and should be compliant with the Equality Act 2010 and the Disability Discrimination Acts. While this is likely to be the case for new-build accommodation, many refuge organisations are situated in rather difficult old buildings with poor access. As far as possible, premises for domestic violence services should be adapted to be fully accessible in all ways. (In best practice, this might include, for example, providing a fully adapted flat or bungalow for refuge users.)

- Ideally domestic violence organisations should go above and beyond what is required under the legislation (which is a basic minimum).

- Domestic violence organisations need to work to increase awareness among disabled women regarding domestic violence services. Unless disabled women are specifically 'targeted' in domestic violence publicity and outreach, they may not know that accessible facilities are available.

- Thus, the development of accessible services needs to go hand-in-hand with a wider 'reaching out' exercise by domestic violence organisations specifically, both with other service providers and with users of services. This may include domestic violence organisations engaging in advertising, meeting with disabled women's groups and individuals, holding events on disability and domestic violence, and working in partnership with local disability organisations.

- Abused disabled women do not form a homogeneous group, but come from diverse backgrounds, and have different types of impairments, needs and life experiences. Thus, publicity information needs to take on these different needs, to be provided in different formats, and to be (a) accurate, and (b) appropriately detailed.

- There needs to be recognition that the use of accessible formats may require lengthy communication and cannot be done quickly.

- Reaching out needs to be to all disabled women, including BMER women and lesbians and other minority women experiencing abuse.

- Disabled women should always be fully consulted with, and involved at some level at least, in the provision of services.

- Domestic violence organisations could usefully aim to employ a specialist disability advocate.

- Allowance should also be made for the fact that a disabled woman considering moving into refuge accommodation may need a prior visit to assess whether her needs will be adequately met (for example, whether her PA can be accommodated, or another PA provided for her).

- Attempts should be made to avoid isolation for disabled women resident in domestic violence organisations (for example, if the adapted suite is on the ground floor away from other refuge residents and communal meeting areas). There needs to be a commitment to encourage interaction and to make shared spaces accessible.

- Both refuge workers and residents who are not disabled may need to work on demystifying disability and addressing the social model. This may entail breaking down the 'taboo', talking about disability issues in the refuge, honestly and openly addressing these and overcoming anxieties that non-disabled workers and women may have about 'getting it wrong'.

- Managements need to embed the issue in their action plans, operational priorities and budgets, in order that the needs of disabled women become a fundamental concern in domestic violence organisations.

- Disabled women need to be represented in the work and paid staff of the domestic violence organisation, for example as helpline, refuge and outreach workers (including, where possible, minority women and lesbians). In order to enable change to occur most effectively, disabled women need, where possible, to be represented at management level in local domestic violence projects and also regionally and nationally in Women's Aid.

- Women's Aid national office needs to continue to promote best practice and to embed attention to disability as a core issue in domestic violence work, through dissemination of these recommendations and action upon them, together with associated resources.

- Issues for disabled women need to continue to be included in good practice guidelines and national service standards (as now developed by Women's Aid), along with other equality and diversity issues.

Further detailed recommendations for disabled people's organisations

- Disabled people's organisations with a relevant work programme need to start to take on domestic violence issues and to regard such issues as one part of their brief.

- In order to do so, secure resourcing should be sought for all disabled people's and disability organisations, since funding is currently very precarious for many.

- Awareness-raising about domestic violence needs to take place throughout the disability field, as many disabled people's organisations are not aware of gender issues or of violence against women.

- Disability organisations need to develop their own domestic violence policies.

- Training is likely to be needed on routine enquiry about domestic violence and how to respond appropriately to disclosures.

- Awareness-raising needs also to include posters, leaflets and awareness-raising events put on by the disability organisation, possibly in partnership.

- Disabled people's and disability organisations need also to consider employing dedicated women's workers with domestic violence knowledge.

- Organisations providing support and advocacy need, where possible, to offer a choice of male or female advocates to those using their services.

- Partnership and inter-agency work with local domestic violence organisations, forums and services is vital in this context.

- In general, there is a need to raise the profile of the issue of domestic violence and abuse, including by intimate carers, as a fundamental one within the work of relevant disabled people's organisations and the disabled people's movement.

Additional recommendations for the statutory sector

There are four overarching areas that the statutory sector could improve upon to better meet the needs of disabled women experiencing domestic abuse:

- The first is the adoption of adequate definitions.

- The second is the development and implementation of better methods of recording and monitoring. At the moment, little data collection is carried out on this issue.

- The third is the provision of services and guidance throughout relevant statutory sector agencies (possibly on a multi-agency basis).

- The fourth is the provision of professional training and public education on abused disabled women's needs and the services available.

In more detail, these include:

- Attention to the needs of disabled women who have experienced domestic abuse should be mainstreamed in the statutory sector in relevant work plans, budgets and policies.

- The sensitive use of the government *No Secrets* national guidance (Department of Health and Home Office 2005) should be helpful in terms of supporting women experiencing domestic violence, as further discussed in the next chapter.

- As part of the single equality duty under the Equality Act 2010 (as discussed in detail in Chapter 8 as well as Chapter 5), relevant agencies should be able to develop action plans and objectives that encompass disability, with input from disabled women, and to ensure that the needs of abused disabled women are included in these.

- Both service provision and related guidance need to aim to give the disabled woman experiencing abuse as much control as possible, and balance protection and risk assessment with a women's empowerment approach.

- Statutory agencies may be able to set up, and benefit from the advice of, disability advisory groups of disabled domestic violence activists/ consultants to advise on improving services, with payment or at least compensation for members where possible (as also discussed in the next chapter).

- Networks and partnerships between the relevant statutory and voluntary sector agencies providing services need to be developed as required to address disability and domestic abuse, using collectively agreed definitions and service approaches.

- In best practice, such definitions would include the statement that intimate violence is a common occurrence for disabled women; is sometimes perpetrated by family members in a carer situation, or by PAs and paid carers; may be experienced by a range of women (including BMER women and lesbians); and may very well include financial abuse and sexual and psychological violence.

- Thus, current definitions of domestic violence used for all women may need to be expanded and adapted to include disabled women's needs in relation particularly to who perpetrates the violence and how.

- Disabled women, as noted above, should never be placed in residential institutions as a solution to domestic abuse (unless they request this outcome).

- Welcoming and accessible temporary accommodation and homelessness provision (as well as refuges) are particularly required to enable abused women to leave violent situations. Support may also be needed for women to get to and use the accommodation. Such facilities need to be advertised, where they exist, so that disabled women are aware that options exist under the homelessness legislation.

- Fair access to care services (and its successor schemes in the future), practice guidance and eligibility criteria regulate access to social and support services for disabled people. The threshold criteria for the various levels of eligibility need to be set so that abused disabled women will qualify for help.

- Best practice includes working with local adult care services to put in place good practice guidance on community care packages and domestic violence (possibly agreed on a multi-agency basis). There should then be processes in place to ensure that the guidance is fully implemented and that agencies know about it.

- Disabled women experts, and both domestic violence and disability organisations, need to be consulted thoroughly about such guidance.

- Care planning is likely to need to be flexible so that women's care packages are portable, where possible. This may be assisted by reciprocal agreements between different local authority areas to avoid disputes in individual cases about who is responsible.

- In localities where it may be too ambitious to agree multi-agency guidance on care packages, social care/adult services staff need at the least to be provided with training on how to respond to disabled women who are experiencing domestic violence.

Being aware of abuse by personal assistants and paid carers

- There is a need to acknowledge and be vigilant about potential abuse by paid carers and PAs (in both the statutory and voluntary sector agencies).

- Sensitive and non-judgemental investigation is required, according to the relevant procedures. It is important not automatically to believe the carer's or PA's account of events, and not to disbelieve or ignore the disabled woman.

- Agencies need to be aware of the difficulties arising under the personalisation agenda where there is domestic abuse. While this system does give disabled people more control, it can be difficult for women experiencing abuse from their PA or paid carer. They may be left without the support and professional help needed to deal with such a problematic issue and may thus live in a situation of fear and extreme vulnerability.

- Mechanisms need to be developed to ensure disabled women have access to guidance about such situations, including peer support groups, buddying with other disabled women employing PAs and paid carers, advice-giving websites, and use of the *No Secrets* framework and of agency practice protocols and procedures.

Chapter 8

Strategic Agendas

Incorporating Issues for Disabled Women Experiencing Domestic Violence

In the previous chapters, we have described disabled women's experiences of domestic violence and abuse, the professional and service responses in place, and some ideas for good practice. As we have discussed throughout, it is very clearly the case that, despite good intentions and real attempts to improve by Women's Aid, many domestic violence services still are not able to respond adequately to disabled women coming to them for help. It is even more difficult, very often, for disabled people's organisations. With the exception of some pioneering disabled women's groups and individual disabled women activists, disability organisations overall have still scarcely begun to tackle the issue. Statutory agencies also tend to respond inadequately. True, there have been some improvements over recent years and, as discussed in the previous chapter, our research was able to identify recommendations for good practice to assist with further improvements and to try to ensure that abused disabled women get a better deal in the future. Hence there is hope.

It takes willpower to turn hope into reality, however. Without the political will to make changes more broadly and in the absence of a wider coordinated effort across the board, better services here and there will remain isolated 'one-offs'. National and local coordination and commitment are key, together with the further development of attention to the issue at the political and policy level, as outlined also in Chapter 6. Women's Aid nationally is trying just such a coordinated policy response, attempting to ensure that all refuges and support services under its umbrella provide accessible and sympathetic services and that workers have disability equality training. These attempts have not yet gone far enough, clearly, but the effort is there and this study was specifically commissioned by Women's Aid nationally to help to meet the gaps. Although little change is yet evident, some umbrella disability organisations have also made a start on wider coordinated action. It must be repeated, though, that the current cutbacks in public expenditure may threaten these advances. Already, various domestic violence projects have hit the dust, as have some disability groups which have had their funding terminated. It appears that the good practice advances that came out of our study and which we highlighted in the previous chapter are being jeopardised currently, and will be further jeopardised in the future, as disabled women, victims of domestic violence including children, and other vulnerable individuals and groups face the full impacts of new funding strategies, reduced budgets and mandated cutbacks which dwarf those of previous generations.

Where wider strategies and strategic plans exist across the diverse services needed and across local areas to support provision, and where these strategies are coordinated and lead to commissioning policies on the new approaches and services required, some of these difficulties can be overcome. To move forward, we need to advocate for the development of such strategic commitment by the national bodies concerned, by both local statutory and voluntary agencies – and by national and local government. In our research, we developed a substantial raft of recommendations specifically to inform this strategic agenda (and additional to the recommendations for good practice in agencies described in the previous chapter). These latter guidelines, which we outline on a general level here, will assist in leading towards improved commissioning, provision, regulation and coordination of services. No matter how this or any subsequent government chooses to carry these out, they remain an underpinning framework that must be in place if disabled, abused women are to be adequately helped and supported. Fragmentation, for example by the localisation agenda, makes it far harder to address hidden problems such as this one, or to hear silenced voices.

In the rest of this chapter, we address these wider strategic issues and consider whether niches exist in strategic agendas, policies and the commissioning of services that could be helpfully developed further. How can we ensure that disability and domestic violence are part of such local and national strategic agendas, and then stay on them? How can we ensure that issues for disabled women facing abuse are integrated into multi-service provision and commissioning in the future and how can they be raised when local communities and volunteers are left to carry the can? How can we move beyond piecemeal services and good practice confined in isolated pockets within a general sea of lack of attention and the overlooking of abused disabled women's needs? The answer seems to be: with great difficulty. However, the discussions throughout this chapter may be of help.

Some basics for strategic agendas

Basically, the overall issues to be taken on in addressing the strategic approach and strategic agendas both locally and nationally are quite straightforward. Put simply, they involve two interlocking and complementary issues. The first is making sure that there is an integration of domestic violence into all strategic work and policy development on disability. The second is the reverse: making sure that disabled women's needs are integrated into all domestic violence strategic work. These points may seem self-evident, but they are hard to achieve, as strategy and policy officers with a commitment to the issue can attest.

Most importantly within this effort, there are two further underlying issues of commitment and principle, which we have returned to again and again throughout this book. The first is the adoption of a gendered approach to, and understanding of, domestic violence, including an understanding that same-sex couples and carers can buy into the belittling and abuse of other women. The importance of a gendered perspective is of key importance in developing domestic violence responses at the strategic level to disability, as it is to everything else about the issue. Secondly, a principled, nuanced and careful usage of the social model of disability needs to be part of all strategic and policy work, as discussed in Chapter 6. In general, the literature points out that an intersectional approach is needed to all issues of oppression and discrimination to avoid simplistic responses (see Thiara and Gill 2010). This is certainly the case in terms of understanding the situation of abused disabled women and developing strategic responses. Thus, policy- and strategy-makers need a nuanced understanding that blends both the gendered nature of domestic violence and the social model of disability, along with issues of social class, poverty, immigration, religion or belief, potential racism, heterosexism, ageism and so on (most of which are also identified under the equality legislation).

Within these wider frameworks, there are likely to be at least two strands of work that need a strategic overview, in order to promote the good practice we have already outlined. They are, namely, improving service and policy responses on the one hand and, on the other, providing professional training and raising awareness among disabled women, agencies and the public.

What we did in the study to investigate these strategic and commissioning issues

The issues for strategic and commissioning work are rather different from those for developing good practice in agencies. During our study, as we note in our description of the methodology used, we carried out a special set of additional interviews that focused on strategic and commissioning frameworks and agendas in terms of domestic violence and disabled women. These included interviews with domestic violence inter-agency projects, with a local authority disability commissioning manager and with Women's Aid nationally as the principal provider of domestic violence services in England. We also interviewed two domestic violence strategy coordinators, a (then) Local Area Agreement strategy officer, and two disability consultants who were advisers to the police and other agencies on disability issues. Further, we interviewed representatives from the Home Office, the Department of Health, and the Equality and Human Rights Commission. Additional documentary information was widely collected on commissioning guidance and on policies and strategic plans. We also did a 'count' of the inclusion of disability and domestic violence in relevant policy documents and strategies. Recommendations on strategic development were then drawn out of these interviews and related secondary research.

Importance of the strategic, partnership and commissioning agendas

To meet the currently unmet needs of disabled women experiencing domestic violence, good practice in the relevant agencies is essential, as discussed in the previous chapters. However, the development of such practice often depends crucially, as noted above, on the wider strategic and partnership agenda, both nationally and in the relevant local area, because policy tends now to be developed in response to 'policy drivers' coming from government, though with a lessening emphasis by the present government on performance indicators.

Strategically, therefore, the issue of domestic violence for disabled women needs to be part of all relevant strategic agendas and monitoring systems so that, first, it is addressed at the strategic level and, secondly, there are then mechanisms for ensuring that the outcomes of this addressing are in fact carried out. Without policy drivers of these types, abused disabled women's needs are likely to be forgotten or ignored as they have been so many times in the past. If, however, they become part of the relevant national and local mechanisms governing both local statutory and voluntary/third sector services, and if it can be recognised that domestic violence shores up most other social problems for women that are seen in isolation by government, such as the lack of social mobility for many or poor mental health and problems of substance misuse, then a big step forward has been taken. But such a step is rarely enough on its own. The issue of domestic abuse of disabled (amongst other) women then needs to be flagged at a sufficient priority level within these systems and strategies developed to ensure that action is taken by local authorities, health bodies, the police, Women's Aid and so on. Merely a passing mention in government plans and strategies – as often happens, possibly for reasons of being 'seen' to be aware of the issue – rarely makes any difference. There need to be attached service obligations, regularly monitored, and the issue needs to be high enough up the priority agenda that things are done about it.

One of our interviewees was a domestic violence strategy coordinator working across a local authority area to develop area-wide policies on domestic violence. Working all the time at this strategic level, she had this to say:

> Strategic partnership working is essential because, obviously, domestic violence work can't be delivered by any one organisation – it crosses lots of agencies, as oppression issues do generally. So there is a whole range of strategic documents that you need to get it into. And relevant partnerships, or plans like the Equality and Diversity Strategy that most local authorities have. Hate crime strategies… You try to ensure that it goes into all those relevant plans…

These plans and partnerships change frequently as new policies, or new local or central government initiatives, come into play, or when one of the many policy reorganisations is carried out locally. But all the relevant ones at any given time that include domestic violence need further to include domestic violence against disabled women. In particular, this needs to be the case in terms of ensuring that disability and domestic violence services are part of the relevant commissioning frameworks, so that effective services are then successfully brought on stream.

While local and national strategic frameworks continue regularly to be modified in this way, they may also be cancelled or replaced, and may completely disappear or be substantially remodelled by the new government initiatives. It is not possible, therefore, to discuss strategic and partnership agendas comprehensively in this chapter with any degree of confidence that they will still be there and relevant in the next few years. Thus, a few current examples only are included in the following sections, rather than a comprehensive coverage. While many of the policy frameworks overlap with each other to some extent, those mentioned briefly here are loosely divided into national and local categories.

Similarly, there is a wide variety of commissioning frameworks for different services and these also constantly change. Domestic violence and disability should be prioritised in these where relevant, including, where possible or appropriate, in service specifications, invitations to tender, funding and tender terms of reference, and service contracts. Achieving such attention and prioritisation in commissioning can only happen, of course, where capacity exists among the officers and local authorities concerned to take up, make a commitment to, and conduct the required work:

> But I think the key thing is to get it into service commissioning…you know the move towards commissioning arrangements now, commissioning services from different sources. You need to develop goodwill by partnership working in terms of both commissioning and services for agencies and there's a move in the last couple of years to get domestic violence in at a commissioning level. So an example of that…here is that domestic violence is in the…agreements with Accident and Emergency Services and Maternity Services. This will require them to work with ourselves to ensure that midwives are trained, etc…and that will include domestic violence and disabled women. (Domestic violence and disability strategy officer)

It is also important to ensure that adequate monitoring and recording of domestic violence as it affects disabled women is conducted both locally and nationally – in Department of Health, Ministry of Justice and Home Office figures and statistics for example, as well as by national Women's Aid and disability organisations. If there is no national data kept on disabled women and domestic violence, then it is difficult to make a case for service provision.

The *Safeguarding Adults* and *No Secrets* agendas

The *No Secrets* guidance (Department of Health and Home Office 2005) gives inter-agency guidelines, as noted in the previous chapter on good practice, to local authorities responsible for investigating and taking action when an adult at risk (formerly a 'vulnerable adult') is suffering abuse. Operating in parallel with child protection procedures, these include a multi-agency approach and investigation framework leading to the assessment of the needs of the adult concerned and the provision of protection where needed. Local authorities have developed their own policies building on government guidance, and such guidance is clearly applicable in cases of domestic violence, in that abused women are certainly at risk. However, the guidelines may need to be adapted and used sensitively with abused disabled women because, unlike some other groups at risk, such as adults with severe learning difficulties or dementia, they are functioning independently, with the help of care packages where required, and could continue to do so providing the abuse was removed. (Some of the problems with this programme were also discussed in Chapter 6.)

Most of the disabled women involved in our study had not in fact found safeguarding assistance to be of much help precisely because it was insensitively applied. For example, it had sometimes resulted in institutional accommodation being provided against the disabled woman's will, when all she needed was protection from domestic abuse. Adult services, it could be argued, under safeguarding, have a duty to help abused disabled women in distress, but wider supportive strategic frameworks and relevant services will need to be in place for this to be effective.

The Violence Against Women and Girls National Action Plan

In 2010, the coalition government launched a 'Strategic Narrative' on violence against women and girls, following on from and replacing the previous strategy that was developed after extensive consultation by the last government. As noted in Chapter 5, the coalition government's replacement strategy has been accompanied since March 2011 by a *Call to End Violence Against Women and Girls: Action Plan* (HM Government 2011). Prevention is ostensibly at the heart of the plan, as well as provision of adequate levels of support, working in partnership, and improved risk identification. The Action Plan contains commitments on funding rape crisis centres, tackling female genital mutilation, establishing domestic violence homicide reviews and so on, with a focus on awareness-raising, early identification and early intervention. However, it mentions disabled women only once, in passing, as part of its section on who might experience violence.

In fact, in follow-up work to our study, conducted in 2011, it was not possible to find significant references to disabled women experiencing domestic violence and abuse in any of the government's strategic commitments on violence against women. In general, on domestic violence specifically, there appear to be few or no mentions of disabled women in any important strategic documents, for example the Department of Health's handbook for health professionals *Responding to Domestic Abuse* (2005). Disability might be mentioned in definitions, but there is little sign of concrete action, actual proposals for service response or recommendations attached to such cursory mentions.

The *National Plan on Domestic Violence* (see Home Office 2005), initiated by the last Labour government, currently provides specialist domestic violence courts, independent domestic violence advisers (IDVAs), multi-agency risk assessment conferences (MARACs) to address the most serious domestic violence cases, and the beginning of Coordinated Community Responses to domestic violence. While these provisions are being reviewed, and may be cut back, by the present coalition government, they have been highly significant over the last few years and will continue, on some level at least, to be so. It is therefore of some import that none of the related government documents appear to mention disabled women.

If these, or future, national policies and strategies are to be effective, our study suggested that it is important to point out again and again how essential it is that the needs of abused disabled women are included in them and that these needs are attached to concrete provisions and mentioned specifically in action plans.

Local policies and strategies

In terms of local strategic work, it is worth reiterating the importance of, first, the inclusion of domestic violence in all relevant equality and diversity strategies, schemes, frameworks, action plans, objectives and agendas; and, second, the inclusion of disability in all domestic violence and crime reduction strategies, agendas and frameworks, as we have previously discussed in terms of good practice in Chapter 7. Our interviews in the study pointed out time and again the two-way nature of this key strategic and policy commitment: domestic violence as part of all relevant disability policy work; disability as part of all domestic violence work.

Domestic violence in the equalities agenda

Work needs to be carried out continuously to raise the profile of domestic violence in equalities work. Over recent years, equality work has been governed by the development of national legislation, previously including the disability equality duty and the gender equality duty which were established from 2006. Since the introduction of the disability equality duty, local disabled people needed to be involved in, and to support (that is, not merely be consulted about), the development of local disability equality schemes, and this meant, of course, disabled women as well as disabled men. These duties provided obvious and important routes for potentially highlighting the needs of abused disabled women.

The Equality Act 2010 superseded the previous legislation, as we have noted throughout. Under this Act, public agencies, local councils and other bodies were given a unified single public sector equality duty to replace the preceding multiple duties, although the strands of these duties were encompassed within it. While this provision could potentially weaken the previous disability equality and gender equality duties to some extent, both are still clearly identified as components, and focused policy attention to both remains a requirement. Thus, the single duty will still be able to be used in regard to disability and domestic violence. This may be an area where work could be further developed on this issue, both now and in the future, as equality duties and schemes are refined, reviewed or replaced.

International human rights statutes and instruments and the national human rights agenda can also be used in representing the needs and interests of disabled women who have experienced domestic violence.

Disability in local strategies on domestic violence or violence against women and girls

Many local authorities currently have independent stand-alone domestic violence strategies, as noted, which are now likely to disappear or to be replaced with violence against women and girls strategies because that is the national terminology currently adopted by government. Good practice is clearly for the needs of disabled women to feature, both now and in the future, in these types of strategies, in priorities and objectives for action arising from them, and in the resultant action plans themselves.

However, in our study, we found that very few domestic violence strategies in operation around the country in 2009–2010 included much in the way of reference to disabled women. While some did not mention disability at all a majority did so, but only briefly in definitions or overall statements about domestic violence. In detail, out of 124 district, unitary, county and metropolitan authority domestic violence strategies analysed, disabled women were not mentioned at all in 21. In 77, disabled women were mentioned but only in general definitions.

A minority, just 26 out of the 124 (fewer than 1 in 5), included mention in actual plans committing local agencies to engaging in any action at all on the issue. Where it was included, the action was normally minimal or of a general nature, for example 'to have a commitment to improving services for disabled women', which does not commit anyone to anything in reality, since it is too vague.

A good practice example: disability advisory groups

It can be helpful for agencies and partnerships evolving action plans to be advised on a strategic level by disability advisory groups of disabled consultants. A disabled women consultant on disability issues whom we interviewed explained that:

> There is the Disability Independent Advisory Group of the Metropolitan Police, DIAG. It's a group of several people and there was a small group of us within that, about four or five of us, who are disabled and who are particularly concerned with domestic violence. We raise issues about the fact that violence happens against disabled women (and men) in the home, sometimes from people who are family members in a carer situation. And so does financial abuse and psychological abuse and so on, as we know. And we assist in writing guidelines and policies.

This work is hard and demanding, however, for disabled women and it is poor practice to expect it to be done without any compensation or support being offered. At such meetings, the police and other officers attending are undoubtedly being paid but the disabled consultants may not be. The consultant quoted above went on to say:

> But it's a real uphill struggle. You can feel like you are working and working and giving your time and everything else and nothing much changes. Of course we had to attend for no money and in our free time…

Thus, good practice would include payment or compensation, expenses and support to attend. It is also poor practice if an isolated disabled woman has to conduct this work on her own without support, as our respondent pointed out:

> In these advisory groups there can sometimes just be one disabled woman, working with loads of police officers and social workers to write guidance, hopefully based on the social model of disability and human rights perspective, for the police on how to deal with abuse against so-called 'vulnerable adults'.

This outcome is clearly to be guarded against and could be viewed as discriminatory to the disabled woman concerned.

A good practice example: Leeds

The Leeds City Council Domestic Violence Team, formerly the Leeds Inter-Agency Project (LIAP), has worked extensively with partner agencies to develop, until 2011, a recurring three-year domestic violence strategy action plan. This action plan for the city integrated action points on issues for various marginalised groups of women. Disabled women and minority ethnic women were specifically named as groups for whom services must be developed.

In delivering the strategy, 35 agencies had developed domestic violence action plans by 2009–2010. As a 'minimum standard' in their action plan, each agency had then committed to ensure that their services were accessible to disabled women. Thus, the issue became integrated into planning and into the work agendas of the council and of other agencies. Work plans had to include action on producing information in a range of formats, on sending staff on training, and on access issues in terms both of physical barriers, and of attitudinal and structural barriers for disabled women within the organisations concerned.

The Leeds project has found it was useful to have a dedicated worker focusing on the issue of disability. This worker was able to ensure that these issues were integrated at a strategic level so that the work was then carried out and embedded into the work of other agencies. An inter-agency worker explained that:

> this idea of having basic work on disabled women and domestic violence as a minimum standard is really important because that ensures that your broader work around domestic violence includes disabled women as part of your minimum standards and that it's naturally in there all the time. And we do the same with BMER women's issues as well.

This work has developed into the Leeds Domestic Violence Services Minimum Standards Quality Mark. There are several levels to this 'quality mark' with requirements to be achieved for each one. For level one, agencies need to demonstrate awareness of the needs of vulnerable groups, including disabled women and BMER abused women, and training and accessibility. For level two, they need to show how they actually respond effectively in terms of practice to these groups. The domestic violence quality mark can then be incorporated into local commissioning frameworks for agencies and into the relevant service agreements, so that agencies as a consequence are able to use the achievement of a domestic violence 'minimum standards quality mark' in their publicity and grant applications. In 2010, for example, the Leeds City Council Domestic Violence Team quality-marked all of the children's centres in Leeds.

In summary, then, this example of best practice includes the incorporation of domestic violence and disability into all relevant local plans and strategies, the development of domestic violence minimum standards and the application of graded quality marks which agencies work to attain (for example, on accessibility, training and direct service provision for disabled women).

Most local areas might not be able to achieve such highly developed action plans due to the lack of specialist workers to pioneer the work. However, domestic violence coordinators or strategy coordinators now exist in various localities with well-developed and embedded domestic violence services. These coordinators and others may have capacity to develop this work further in the future. Areas without such capacity might still be able to begin the process in partnership with other local agencies.

Detailed recommendations for strategic development

In the previous chapter, we presented our good practice recommendations in detail, after a more general discussion. The same format is used in this chapter. We present here the detailed recommendations on strategic development that emerged from our study, and that we have discussed in general above. As in the previous chapter, we use a bullet-point form, laying the recommendations out in sections, for easy visibility and access by busy practitioners and policy-makers. In more detail, then, the recommendations for strategic development identified in the study were as follows.

General strategic and commissioning frameworks

- All relevant strategic agendas and commissioning frameworks should include a section on domestic violence in general, and on responding to disabled women's experience of abuse in particular.

- These would be expected to include all relevant joint strategic partnerships, strategic assessments, commissioning intentions, commissioning terms of reference and relevant commissioning frameworks, while these continue to exist and as they develop and change.

- The issue of disability and domestic violence needs to be flagged at a sufficient priority level to ensure that policy responses follow, and to be included in all relevant national and local performance monitoring within these frameworks, while this monitoring continues.

- Monitoring, data collection and recording of domestic violence and disability need to be integrated into all relevant local and national strategy documents, so that reliable data on numbers of disabled women experiencing domestic abuse begins to be available.

- Government plans and strategies (for example, developments in the Action Plan on *Violence Against Women and Girls*, as discussed) need in future to address the issue of disabled women.

- International Human Rights statutes and instruments and the national human rights agenda could also be used in representing the needs of abused disabled women.

- The needs of disabled women experiencing domestic violence should feature in the planned development of the Supporting People programme, in future financial criteria for funding it, and in any subsequent funding frameworks (in terms of both residential provision and floating support). Conversely, ring-fencing of some of this funding for domestic abuse work is actually being removed.

- The single public sector equality duty (replacing the former disability and gender equality duties) – and further equality requirements that may in turn replace this or come into play in the future – are important, as we have noted, in terms of the needs of disabled abused women. These needs should be mentioned, and where possible highlighted, in policies relating to this duty for public sector organisations, and in the development of equality schemes and action plans in terms of both disability and gender, so that the new unified equality duty does not weaken the previous, more specific provision.

Domestic violence strategies and the equality agenda

- All equalities and diversity work should include attention to the issue of domestic violence.

- Strategies on violence against women and girls and against domestic violence are important vehicles for work on disability and domestic violence. The needs of disabled women need to be specifically addressed in these plans. A mere mention of disability is not enough.

- In particular, local strategies should incorporate the need for actual service provision for abused disabled women.

Thus, there are two general principles:

- Disability needs to be included in all domestic violence strategies, agendas and frameworks developed by local authorities and strategic partnerships.

- Similarly, domestic violence and disabled women's needs should feature in all diversity and equality strategies, agendas and frameworks, both locally and nationally.

Domestic violence quality marks and minimum standards

- Local relevant strategies and action plans (and relevant agencies themselves) should consider developing domestic violence minimum standards, to include meeting the needs of disabled women.

- In best practice, services could then qualify for graded 'quality marks' which agencies could attain (for example, on accessibility, training and direct service provision for disabled women) and could subsequently use in their publicity and documents.

Domestic violence organisations

- Our study strongly recommended that the future of specialist domestic violence services themselves needs to be ensured in general, both at present and within future funding regimes and the Supporting People programme in particular.

- Thus, relevant strategic instruments across local areas need to include domestic violence service provision and, within that, a commitment to provide services for abused disabled women in an accessible way.

Disabled people's organisations

- Overall funding for disabled people's organisations remains very vulnerable and inadequate, and needs to be secured on a general level to ensure that they can attempt to take on the needs of disabled abused women.

- Umbrella groups and partnerships in the disability field could consider attempting to promote the strategic inclusion of services for disabled women experiencing domestic violence in the work of disabled people's organisations and disability services with a relevant brief.

- Disabled experts and activists may be able to offer advice services, for example by participating in disability advisory groups advising local authorities and in local strategic development, with payment or compensation for their work where possible.

Chapter 9

Conclusions

This book has represented the voices of disabled women in two ways – both as research respondents and as contributing authors steeped in activism and campaigning. Hence it has an authenticity that merits a wide readership. The importance of its message, too, with its potentially life-and-death impact, commands attention. Our thanks go to the courageous and generous women who gave their time to this study. They have faced in their own lives the reality not only of abuse but of ignorance, disbelief and lack of commitment to change. We owe it to them to hear what they have to say and to act upon it.

Empowering disabled women to speak in their own voices has challenged a number of commonly accepted definitions, statistics and assumptions – for example, that our so-called 'caring society' has the necessary forms of help in place when we are clearly leaving open so many gaping holes in provision. The national Women's Aid definition of domestic abuse (see Chapter 1) sees it as occurring in an 'intimate or family-type relationship', whereas listening to disabled women reminds us that there may be someone in their household who has intimate contact with them but who may be, not a partner, but a paid carer/personal assistant. We also need to become aware that the abuse of disabled women may be up to twice as common even than the abuse of women more generally, meaning that the '1 in 3', '1 in 4' or '1 in 5' that we all have been variously quoting up to now (depending on which source you prefer) may need to step up to '1 in 2' where disabled women are concerned. This is not so hard to believe when you think that, amongst one group of disabled women we heard about, talking about abuse outside of this study, every single one had known some kind of abuse as a child – for example, the taxi driver one remembered taking her to school who used to put his hand up her skirt when he lifted her in and out of the cab. This is the reality for many disabled women.

We stated at the opening of this book that our study would be grounded in the social model of disability – that is, in the view that it is society's attitude, along with the barriers this creates, that is disabling rather than physical impairment itself. Our study findings and the wisdom of our disabled contributors have established beyond doubt that abuse and the lack of appropriate services to deal with it are further disabling. The individual is let down again and again – she is failed by others and by society more generally. The distressing accounts we offer here of impairment-specific abuse, of women's isolation in the face of that abuse, and of the lack of effective help, should make us all determined to take action for change.

The research study on which this book is largely based was the first national project in England to look at the needs of disabled women who had experienced domestic violence and abuse. Its findings relate the usual sickening accounts of what men, and some women, do to women they are supposed to love and care about. The accounts women shared of their experiences were made even more distressing by the ways in which their impairment had almost always been used against them to create additional ways to abuse, both verbally through name-calling and belittling in relation to the impairment, and physically through exploiting the woman's need for assistance and relative helplessness without it. Yet, this power dynamic plays straight into stereotypes of the selfless carer and the asexual disabled woman – no one would believe this carer was abusive and no one stops to think that this woman has the right to a violence-free sex- and love-life.

A further compounding of the vulnerability of disabled women to abuse comes about, ironically, through the personalisation agenda. Worthy as it may be to accord disabled people greater control over their own lives through direct payments and the right to select and employ their own carers, no one would dream of taking on employment responsibilities in a formal organisation without an entire human resources department to back them up. Yet the disabled person, if faced with a paid carer who is exploitative, inappropriate or downright abusive, currently has no back-up service of any kind to support or assist them. When adult social services tend to believe and side with the carer rather than the disabled employer of that carer, you have a real recipe for trouble and, in the worst cases, severe danger. Where is adult safeguarding in this context? Our recommendations consequently look to mutual assistance, through buddying or collective support, rather than to statutory sector back-up, but that would be as good or even better if it could be trusted.

This additional issue of carer abuse is one that, to our knowledge, no one is really tackling. The personalisation agenda cannot be said to do much for individual rights or choice if it leads to these new scenarios of abuse. There are few systems for monitoring or responding, very little support for those experiencing abuse at the hands of paid carers, and, commonly, no action taken against those who abuse. Even if dismissed from their employment, they are often free to go on to abuse someone else. If the disabled woman tries to complain, she may risk being seen as refusing care, no matter how difficult her care package was to put in place or how essential it is to her life. The package will come up for review on an annual basis and, in a climate of cuts, privatisation and inadequate regulation, the disabled woman may well fear that her funding will be taken away if she makes a fuss. She thus faces a vicious circle. The more dependent she is upon her carer, the more open she is to abuse.

Looked at more broadly, it is tremendously worrying that professionals are not spotting domestic violence perpetrated against disabled women, and that they certainly are not routinely checking for it. Now that we know how many disabled women and girls are being abused, it is absolutely essential that all professions ask the right questions about violence, that they do so in a sensitive way and that they see the woman on her own – not in the presence of the possible abuser. This means asking the questions of everyone, including professional women (who may actually find it hardest to disclose) and men as well, though this particular study and book have not been about them. The police need to be proactive and to believe women, not wait for referrals from other organisations. Individual police officers, social workers, GPs, district nurses and all the others who come into contact with disabled women need to know where there is accessible emergency accommodation locally or, better still in many cases, how the law can be used to remove an abuser and how other domiciliary care can go straight in to replace the care the abuser was giving. Anyone who works with known domestic violence – including solicitors, GPs and all the caring, health and legal professions – must recognise the potentially life-and-death consequences of revealing information to partners and carers without a woman's permission. Abusers are often plausible and charming and, as we have seen here, they may be carers whom the world puts upon a pedestal and yet who may make a woman's life a living hell.

It is against all professional values and protocols, and also now against the spirit of equality legislation, to ignore domestic violence. Failure to see and failure to respond are both equally dangerous. A disabled woman is doubly or trebly vulnerable – she is open to more frequent and additional forms of abuse, she is trapped in the abuse, the services that could help her do not exist or are not appropriate or she does not get to hear about them, other people automatically side with her abuser (as either a self-sacrificing partner or a paid quasi-professional) and, if she complains, she is calling her entire care package and her independent life into question. Imagine yourself trying to break out of that one. It is truly the stuff of nightmares. Yet, if you are a practitioner or a policy-maker reading this, you can help just by joining together disability and domestic violence in your everyday thinking. It really is that simple.

The biggest change that came about through the introduction of disability equality and gender equality legislation was placing the onus on services to be in place and ready when a disabled and/or female service user came along. It is no longer supposed to be up to the individual to fight their corner. There is a duty on both the statutory and voluntary sectors to have thought about their needs in advance. When the emergency need arises, it happens now – not next week or next month or when we've managed to get the services sorted. Recognition of disabled abused women needs to be embedded in all the responses we make, not added on as an afterthought. This means national policy, local strategy and frontline good practice all having the guidelines in place and acting on them.

Tokenism is still in evidence, notably where disabled women are mentioned in passing, usually in definitions, and then do not feature in detailed policy or practice guidance, as we have discussed in previous chapters. Yet we are not talking about rocket science. Just imagine yourself in a wheelchair, or with limited mobility, or unable to see or unable to hear. How would you learn about domestic violence so that you could conceptualise that it was happening to you or know there were services out there to help you? What if you were lesbian or from a minority ethnic community and feared that the mainstream services would not take you seriously or would not be appropriate for you? Worse than all this, how would you feel if, having finally accessed some services, they fobbed you off because there were no accessible routes to escape available or because your abusive partner was also your carer so you could not be left on your own?

Disability services understand these complexities of coping and caring, while domestic violence services understand that it is hard to face the fact that one is being abused and needs some kind of urgent help. All we have to do is to stitch the two together and we've cracked it. Then we need to get the statutory services, such as the police and social services, to take on board the new, combined understanding and we need everyone to remember this. All the time.

In a rapidly shifting policy context, it is hard to make detailed recommendations. But whether it is central government, the local authority, the voluntary sector, the local community or the family that offers most help, some messages remain the same. Abuse does happen to disabled women. There is reason to believe that it happens even more than to other women, and in particularly mean and nasty ways. Services are harder for disabled women to access. They are currently inadequate and poorly adapted to disabled women's needs. These gaps are not hard to fill and they do not require new knowledge. All we have to do is join together two sets of understandings we already have, but which tend to be held in two different sectors within our welfare provision. Although getting it right may involve more work and more resources, there is a legislative imperative to provide these – through the single equality duty – and it is also the case that a great deal can be done just by remembering to 'think disability' whenever we are dealing with domestic violence and to 'think abuse' whenever we are dealing with disability. Doing this can mean that all building design, all service specification, all sub-contracting and tendering, all practice protocols and all day-to-day responses are likely to become more appropriate and more effective.

This book has been a long time coming. We ask you to read it, be shocked, get over it, and do something practical to contribute. If you are not sure quite what to do, go and talk to some disabled women. Make sure disabled women have a formal role in or with your organisation, if you are involved with one. Grow strong together and write up, and share, the results. That way good practice spreads. If you are an abused disabled woman, we hope you can access whatever support you need or want, and that the book has been useful.

This book may well have been a distressing read, but it concludes with a message of hope. There are clear and optimistic ways forward in finally taking seriously the needs of disabled women experiencing abuse. We do know what will be of use and we do know what can be done. All we have to do is remember the following:

- No domestic violence services without thinking about disability.

- No disability services without gendering our thinking and remembering abuse.

Appendix

Study Methodology

This multi-methods study was conducted in three stages, each of which built on the one before. In the first stage of the study on which this book is based, wide-ranging consultations were carried out. These included email, telephone and correspondence consultations with disabled abused women nationally through Women's Aid, consultations with a range of relevant disability and domestic violence organisations and their members, and national distribution of publicity through the UK Disabled People's Council, leading to a further publicity drive.

This was followed by a focus group with disabled abused women drawn from across the country, which informed the research design and was conducted in accessible premises with careful attention to the needs of each woman. A data set of 15 interviews with key professionals and activists in women's and disability organisations was then carried out as well as a literature review; and a content analysis of policy and legislation. These exercises helped us to develop ideas for the research and to inform the rest of the study. This initial phase of work was used to develop two national surveys, one of local Women's Aid and domestic violence organisations, and the other of disabled people's organisations.

For both surveys, detailed questionnaires were developed in consultation with disabled women, with the Advisory Group and with Women's Aid, and piloted with three relevant organisations. The research tools were modified accordingly after the pilots. The research instruments collected data on accessibility, aids, adaptations, staff training, services offered, data collection and monitoring of disabled abused women, attitudes to disabled women, multi-agency approaches, liaison between the disability and domestic violence sectors, and other issues and challenges encountered when working with disabled abused women. The survey of domestic violence organisations was sent, with the assistance of Women's Aid, to 350 local domestic violence services within England, identified through Women's Aid lists and UKRefugesonline. This is a computerised database of refuges and services available and includes all local domestic violence organisations, updated twice a year, with new services and changes to contacts updated on an ongoing basis. After repeated written, email and telephone follow-ups and encouragement from Women's Aid through member newsletters, the final responses numbered 133, giving a response rate of 40 per cent. The geographical location of responding domestic violence service providers was spread throughout the country and included some specialist projects which provided services for black and minority ethnic families, or specifically for South Asian or African-Caribbean women. Some responding organisations included several service-providing projects.

The survey of disability organisations was sent out to 348 disabled people's organisations in England, a list which was compiled from numerous sources including the (then) British Association of Disabled People's Organisations. Twenty-six of these agencies had to close during the survey process due to funding crises and the research team was not able to obtain any additional information about them. After extremely time-consuming written, email and telephone follow-up, a total of 126 responses were received, giving a response rate of 39 per cent, although many of these said they did not work on the issue. Both the surveys were analysed using SPSS to draw out percentages and, where appropriate, cross-tabulations across the survey questions (for example, on geographic location, accessibility, disability equality training, equality policies, compliance with disability legislation, dedicated work on domestic violence and disability, and so on).

In the second stage of the study, all research tools, including the schedule and topic guides for the in-depth interviews with disabled women who had experienced domestic violence, were developed by drawing on the findings of the first stage. They were consulted widely in both the disability and domestic violence fields, and also with Women's Aid and the Advisory Group. They were then piloted with three disabled women who had experienced abuse, after which the interview schedules were adapted accordingly. In addition, as required for research in an area of great sensitivity and difficulty, appropriate information flyers, leaflets, confidentiality agreements, consent forms, comprehensive lists of helping agencies, and other support and information materials were developed. The interviews investigated experiences both of abuse and of seeking help from services. As well as collecting some basic demographic information for all interviewees, they focused on the impact of being disabled on the violence experienced, the nature, length and perpetrators of abuse, the woman's ability to respond to the abusive situation, the impact on children, the nature of help-seeking through informal and formal routes, the responses received, advice offered by the interviewees to other disabled abused women, and possibilities for good practice.

In-depth and lengthy interviews were then conducted with 30 abused disabled women ranging in age from 20 to 70 years who had a range of sensory and physical impairments, and came from diverse backgrounds in terms of ethnicity, sexuality and socio-economic status. Twenty-six per cent were over 50 years of age. The interviewees had a range of physical and sensory impairments including visual, mobility and hearing difficulties, and ongoing and degenerative illnesses. Some had become disabled because of domestic violence. They included two lesbians, 27 heterosexuals and one bisexual woman. Twenty were white British, nine came from a range of BMER backgrounds including Turkish, African-Caribbean and South Asian, and one was white Irish. The largest group lived in adapted council accommodation but others lived in owner-occupied, rented or housing association property. Nineteen women had children. Careful attention was paid to each woman's needs, impairments and the extreme sensitivity of the issues during the interview, which was often very long and sometimes distressing. Building the sample was extraordinarily difficult. It was only achieved after repeated and very time-consuming efforts at contact and follow-up over many months.

All interviews were recorded, transcribed and analysed using thematic analysis methods. An initial coding frame developed out of the interview and research questions was applied to the transcripts. Each transcript was read and re-read within the research team, enabling a great deal of familiarisation, to identify emerging themes, to interpret data in a systematic and transparent method, and to ensure the themes were grounded in the data. A framework of key issues and themes was gradually developed out of this initial analysis, along with sub-themes, and data was entered into this from each interviewee. A short summary of each transcript, outlining key information for each narrative, was also developed which allowed for easier cross-checking of data, if required. This framework, grounded in and shaped by women's narratives, enabled the full range of circumstances, experiences and views to be compared both across and within narratives, and for themes and patterns to be identified and further explored.

In the third stage of the study, we built on the findings of this analysis and on the surveys in the first stage regarding existing services and policy to identify examples of good practice. These were investigated through agency interviews and four detailed case studies of organisations which were using elements of best practice. Each case study was conducted with multiple sets of interviews. A further data-set of 17 in-depth interviews were carried out with key officers in statutory agencies, strategic partnerships and commissioning bodies to take advice on the wider strategic and commissioning framework in which UK services for disabled women and domestic violence are set.

Recommendations for good practice and for strategic development were then drawn out, and triangulated with the other data-sets.

The study produced an Interim Report, a Full Report, a separate Executive Summary and a Good Practice Guide. All are available, including in large print, from Women's Aid and translations into BSL have commenced. The study led to a launch conference for strategy level officers nationally through Women's Aid, and a variety of seminars, papers and presentations, including to groups of disabled women, in both this country and internationally. Three academic papers were produced and several smaller professional papers. International liaison has established links with similar research and research groups in various countries including, for example, Sweden, Spain and Australia.

About the Authors

Ruth Bashall

Ruth Bashall has been an active feminist for 35 years, and disability rights activist for over 20 years, working extensively on domestic violence and with disabled women's networks, including the Frida Network, a disabled women's sexual health project. She has worked widely as an independent disability equality trainer and consultant, and, until 2010, was Co-chair of the Disability Independent Advisory Group to the Metropolitan Police Service (a group of Deaf and disabled people advising MPS on policy in relation to disabled people, including on domestic and sexual violence). As Chair of Disability Action Waltham Forest, a disabled people's organisation, she helped set up Stay Safe, a user-led project working on violence against women and institutional violence against disabled people. She is a member of advisory groups to the Ministry of Justice, the Metropolitan Police Authority, and the Equality and Human Rights Commission. In her spare time, she cultivates her garden, listens to the trees and hopes against reason that her grandchildren will grow up to live in a world free from violence.

Brenda Ellis

Brenda Ellis has been involved in women's issues, including domestic violence, for many years. She campaigned for disabled women's inclusion in services provided for those experiencing domestic violence while working at Southwark Women's Centre and Greater London Action on Disability (GLAD), realising that there had been little attention given to disabled women in this area. Brenda was an active member of the United Kingdom Disabled People's Council (UKDPC) Women's Committee and a member of the group which set up the first UK Disability Forum Women's Committee website for disabled women, providing information about domestic violence services. She has been involved in the work of Women's Aid to address inclusion for disabled. She would also like to thank Anne Pridmore for all her campaigning work over many years to get this on the agenda and all the other disabled women who have helped with this work.

Gill Hague

Gill Hague is Professor of Violence Against Women Studies in the Centre for Gender and Violence Research, School for Policy Studies, University of Bristol, UK. She was a founder member, with Ellen Malos, in 1990, of this Centre, formerly the Violence Against Women Research Group, which has had, over 20 years, a pioneering role in establishing activist-based violence against women research in the UK and internationally. Gill has worked on violence against women issues for nearly 40 years as an activist, a researcher, an academic and a practitioner. She has produced over 100 publications on violence against women, including several books, and has worked internationally on the issue in many countries of the world including India, Uganda, South Africa, Canada, Iraqi Kurdistan and Mexico. She regarded it as a great privilege to work on this first-ever UK study of disabled women and domestic violence.

Audrey Mullender

Audrey Mullender is Principal of Ruskin College in Oxford, an adult residential college offering further and higher education to second-chance learners. She is Emeritus Professor of Social Work at the University of Warwick and is an Academician of the Social Sciences. She has researched and written for 20 years on domestic abuse as it relates to women, children and men, with a strong emphasis on what can be done to make a difference.

Ravi Thiara

Ravi Thiara is Principal Research Fellow at the Centre for the Study of Safety and Well-being at University of Warwick, UK. Over the last 25 years, she has conducted extensive research and evaluation, training and service development in the violence against women field, in the UK and overseas. Ravi has a particular interest and expertise in violence issues for children, child contact and post-separation abuse, gendered violence within black and minority ethnic communities, and issues for abused disabled women. She has published widely on these issues. In addition, she has written and conducted research on the Indian diaspora in South Africa, bride price and marriage rights in Uganda, and black and minority ethnic youth in the UK.

References

ABS (2004) *Sexual Assault in Australia: A Statistical Overview.* Canberra: Australian Bureau of Statistics.

Association of Chief Police Officers (ACPO) and National Policing Improvement Agency (NPIA) (2008) *Guidance on Investigating Domestic Abuse.* Wyboston: NPIA. Available at www.acpo.police.uk/documents/crime/2008/2008004CRIIDA01.pdf, accessed on 6 September 2011.

Barron, J. (2009) *The Survivor's Handbook.* Available at www.womensaid.org.uk/domestic-violence-survivors-handbook.asp?section=0001000100080001, accessed on 10 October 2011.

Bashall, R. (2006) Speech at EAVES/Lilith Conference on Disabled Women and Abuse, London.

BCODP Women's Committee (1995) 'A charter of rights.' *Women's Committee Newsletter,* Spring. London: British Council of Organisations of Disabled People.

Begum, N. (1990) *Burden of Gratitude: Women with Disabilities Receiving Personal Care. Social Care Perspectives and Practice.* MA Dissertation, University of Warwick.

Begum, N. (1992) 'Disabled Women and the Feminist Agenda.' In H. Hinds, A. Phoenix and J. Stacey (eds) *Working Out: New Directions for Women's Studies.* London: Falmer.

Brisenden, S. (1986) 'Independent living and the medical model of disability.' *Disability, Handicap and Society (Disability and Society since 1993)* 1, 2, 173–178.

Brookes, S. (2010) *Disability, Hostility and Vulnerability.* Briefing to Disability Hate Crime Network, London.

Browne, S.E., Connors, D. and Stern, N. (eds) (1985) *With the Power of Each Breath – A Disabled Women's Anthology.* Berkeley, CA: Cleis Press.

Brownridge, D. (2009) 'Situating research on safety promoting behaviors among disabled and Deaf victims of interpersonal violence.' *Violence Against Women 15,* 9, 1075–1079.

CAADA (2011) 'Domestic Abuse, Stalking and "Honour"-based Violence (DASH) Risk Identification Checklist.' Available at www.caada.org.uk/practitioner_resources/RIC%20 with%20Quick%20Start%20Guidance%20%20Disclaimer%2021052009.pdf, accessed on 8 July 2011.

Campling, J. (1981) *Images of Ourselves.* London: Routledge and Kegan Paul.

Chang, J., Martin, S., Moracco, K., Dulli, L. *et al.* (2004) 'Helping women with disabilities and domestic violence: Strategies, limitations and challenges of domestic violence programs and services.' *Journal of Women's Health 12,* 7, 699–708.

Charlton, J. (1998) *Nothing About Us Without Us: Disability Oppression and Empowerment.* London: University of California Press.

Chenoweth, L. (1997) 'Violence and Women with Disabilities: Silence and Paradox.' In S. Cook and J. Bessant (eds) *Women's Encounters with Violence: Australian Experiences.* California: Sage.

Chenoweth, L. and Clements, N. (2007) *Final Report to Disability Services Queensland on the Disability Sector Quality System Service User Participation Snapshot.* Queensland: Disability Services Queensland.

Chenoweth, L. and Cook, S. (eds) (2001) 'Violence Against Women with Disabilities – Special Issue.' *Violence Against Women 7,* 4.

Cockram, J. (2003) *Silent Voices: Women with Disabilities and Family and Domestic Violence.* Nedlands, WA: People With Disabilities (WA) Inc. Available at www.wwda.org.au/silent1.htm, accessed on 5 July 2011.

Corker, M. and Thomas, C. (2002) 'A Journey around the Social Model.' In M. Corker and T. Shakespeare (eds) *Disability/Postmodernity: Embodying Disability Theory.* London: Continuum.

Crenshaw, K. (1991) 'Mapping the margins: Intersectionality, identity politics and violence against women of color.' *Stanford Law Review 43,* 1241–1245.

Cross, M. (1994) 'Abuse.' In L. Keith (ed.) *Mustn't Grumble: Writing by Disabled Women.* London: The Women's Press.

Cross, M. (1999) *Review of Domestic Violence and Child Abuse: Policy and Practice Issues for Local Authorities and other Agencies.* London: GLAD (Greater London Action on Disability).

Crow, L. (1996) 'Including All of Our Lives: Reviewing the Social Model of Disability.' In J. Morris (ed) *Encounters with Strangers.* London: The Women's Press.

Daily Mail (2010) 'Mother who killed brain damaged son with a heroin overdose gets nine years.' Available at www.dailymail.co.uk/news/article-1244731/Frances-Inglis-guilty-murder.html#ixzz1KTuKhs27, accessed on 8 July 2011.

Daisie Project (2010) *Violence Against Disabled Women Survey.* Glasgow: Daisie Project.

Daley, M. and Lisney, E. (2010) Speech at Million Women Rise, March, London. See www.millionwomenrise.com, accessed on 5 July 2011.

Deaf Women Against Violence/Wise Women (2011) *Information for Deaf Women about Violence Against Women.* Available at www.wisewomen.org.uk/Deaf/index.html, accessed on 6 September 2011.

Department of Health (2005) *Responding to Domestic Abuse: A Handbook for Health Professionals.* London: Department of Health.

Department of Health and Home Office (2005) *No Secrets: Guidance on Developing and Implementing Multi-agency Policies and Procedures to Protect Vulnerable Adults from Abuse.* Available at www.dh.gov.uk/en/publicationsandstatistics/publications/publicationsPolicyAndGuidance/DH_4008486, accessed on 5 July 2011.

Depoy, E., Gilson, S. and Cramer, E. (2003) 'Understanding the Experiences of and Advocating for the Service and Resource Needs of Abused, Disabled Women.' In A. Hans and A. Pat (eds) *Women, Disability and Identity.* London: Sage.

Disabled Peoples' International (2010) *Newsletter,* April. See www.usicd.org/index.cfm/DPI, accessed on 5 July 2011.

DisAbled Women's Network (DAWN) (1986) *Violent Acts Against Disabled People.* Toronto: Disabled Women's Network.

Dobash, R. and Dobash, R. (1992) *Women, Violence and Social Change.* London: Routledge.

Dorian, P.N. (2001). 'So who's left?' *Off Our Backs* October, 19–20.

Dullea, K. and Mullender, A. (1999) 'Evaluation and Empowerment.' In I. Shaw and J. Lishman (eds) *Evaluation and Social Work Practice.* London: Sage.

Ellis, B. (1995) 'The Experiences of Disabled Women: The Disabled Women's Project.' *Social Policy Research Briefing 81.* York: Joseph Rowntree Foundation.

Equality and Human Rights Commission (EHRC) (2009) *Disabled People's Experience of Targeted Violence and Hostility.* London: Office for Public Management.

Equality and Human Rights Commission (EHRC) (2010) 'Public Sector Equality Duty.' Available at www.equalities.gov.uk/equality_act_2010/public_sector_equality_duty.aspx, accessed on 8 July 2011.

Equality and Human Rights Commission (EHRC) (2011a) 'UN Convention on the Rights of Persons with Disabilities.' Available at www.equalityhumanrights.com/human-rights/international-framework/un-convention-on-the-rights-of-persons-with-disabilities, accessed on 8 July 2011.

Equality and Human Rights Commission (EHRC) (2011b) *Hidden in plain sight: Inquiry into disability-related harassment.* Available at www.equalityhumanrights.com/uploaded_files/disabilityfi/ehrc_hidden_in_plain_sight_3.pdf, accessed on 10 October 2011.

Fine, M. and Asch, A. (eds) (1988) *Women with Disabilities: Essays in Psychology, Culture, and Politics.* Philadelphia, PA: Temple University Press.

Flatley, J., Kershaw, C., Smith, K., Chaplin, R. and Moon, D. (2010) *Crime in England and Wales 2009/10. Home Office Statistical Bulletin 12/10.* London: Home Office.

Foreign and Commonwealth Office (2010) *Forced Marriage and Learning Disabilities: Multi-agency Practice Guidelines.* London: FCO. Available at www.fco.gov.uk/forcedmarriage, accessed on 5 July 2011.

French, S. (1996) 'Out of Sight, Out of Mind: The Experience and Effects of a Special Residential School.' In J. Morris (ed.) *Encounters with Strangers.* London: The Women's Press.

Gadd, D., Farrall, S., Dallimore, D. and Lombard, N. (2002) *Domestic Abuse Against Men in Scotland.* Edinburgh: Scottish Executive. Available at www.scotland.gov.uk/Publications/2002/09/15201/9632, accessed on 10 October 2009.

Gangoli, G., Razak, A. and McCarry, M. (2006) *Forced Marriage and Domestic Violence among South Asian Communities in North East England.* Bristol: University of Bristol and Northern Rock Foundation.

Garland-Thompson, R. (2005) 'Feminist disability studies.' *Signs 30,* 21–23.

Gill, A. (2006) 'Patriarchal violence in the name of "honour".' *International Journal of Criminal Justice Sciences 1,* 1, 1–12.

Goode, A. and Ellis, R. (2008) *Public Attitudes Survey.* London: Changing Faces.

Greater London Action on Disability (GLAD) (1997) *'I'm used to it now…': Disabled Women in Residential Care.* London: GLAD.

Guardian (2009) 'Police errors contributed to suicide of tormented mother Fiona Pilkington.' Available at www.guardian.co.uk/uk/2009/sep/28/fiona-pilkington-suicide-mother-police, accessed on 8 July 2011.

Hague, G. and Malos, E. (2005) *Domestic Violence: Action for Change* (3rd Edition). Cheltenham: New Clarion Press.

Hague, G., Mullender, A. and Aris, R. (2003) *Is Anyone Listening?* London: Routledge.

Hague, G., Thiara, R., Magowan, P. and Mullender, A. (2008a) *Making the Links: Disabled Women and Domestic Violence. Full Report.* Bristol: Women's Aid.

Hague, G., Thiara, R., Magowan, P. and Mullender, A. (2008b) *Making the Links: Disabled Women and Domestic Violence. Good Practice Guide.* Bristol: Women's Aid.

Hannaford, S. (1985) *Living Outside Inside. A Disabled Woman's Experience. Towards a Social and Political Perspective.* Berkley, CA: Canterbury Press.

Hassouneh-Phillips, D., McNeff, E., Powers, L. and Curry, M. (2005) 'Invalidation: A central process underlying maltreatment of women with disabilities.' *Women and Health 41,* 1, 33–50.

Healey, D., Howe, K., Humphreys, C., Jennings, C. and Julian, F. (2008) *Building the Evidence: A Report on the Status of Policy and Practice in Responding to Violence against Women with Disabilities in Victoria.* Melbourne: Victorian Women with Disabilities Network Advocacy Information Network.

Hester, M. (2009) *Who Does What to Whom.* Sunderland: Northern Rock Foundation

Hill, F. (1995) *Disabled Women and Domestic Violence Project*. London: Waltham Forest Association of Disabled People.

HM Government (2011) *Call to End Violence Against Women and Girls: Action Plan*. London: Cabinet Office. Available at www.homeoffice.gov.uk/publications/crime/call-end-violence-women-girls, accessed on 5 July 2011.

Home Office (2005) *Domestic Violence: A National Report*. London: Home Office.

Horvath, M. and Kelly, L. (2007) *From the Outset: Why Violence Should be a Core Cross-strand Priority Theme for the Commission for Equality and Human Rights*. London: End Violence Against Women Campaign.

Howe, K. (2007) *Literature Review on Women with Disabilities and Violence Prevention*. Melbourne: Victorian Women with Disabilities Network Advocacy Information Service.

Humphreys, C. and Thiara, R.K. (2002) *Routes to Safety: Protection Issues Facing Abused Women and Children and the Role of Outreach Services*. Bristol: Women's Aid Federation of England.

Hurst, R. (2005) 'Disabled Peoples' International – Europe and the Social Model of Disability.' In C. Barnes and G. Mercer (eds) *The Social Model of Disability: Europe and the Majority World*. Leeds: The Disability Press.

James-Hanman, D. (1994) *Domestic Violence: Help, Advice and Information for Disabled Women*. London: London Borough of Hounslow.

Jansson, K., Coleman, K., Reed, E. and Kaiza, P. (2007) *Home Office Statistical Bulletin 02/07*. London: Home Office.

Jennings C. (2003) 'Violence and women with a disability break down the barriers.' Available at www.wwda.org.au/jennings1.pdf, accessed on 8 July 2011.

Leeds Inter-Agency Project (LIAP) (2002) *Pack for Workshop on Issues for Disabled Women Experiencing Violence from Men They Know*. September. Leeds: LIAP.

London Metropolitan Police (2009) *Safeguarding Adults at Risk Policy and Standard Operating Procedure*. London: Metropolitan Police.

Macleod, J. and Cosgrove, K. (1995) *We're No Exception: Male Violence Against Women with Disability*. Available through Scotland: Convention of Scottish Local Authorities.

Magowan, P. (2003) 'Nowhere to run, nowhere to hide: Domestic violence and disabled women.' *Safe: Domestic Abuse Quarterly 5*, 15–18.

Magowan P. (2004) *The Impact of Disability on Women's Experiences of Domestic Abuse: an Empirical Study into Disabled Women's Experiences of, and Responses to, Domestic Abuse*. ESRC/PhD research, University of Nottingham.

Martin, S., Ray, N., Sotres-Alvarez, D., Kupper, L., Moracco, K. and Dickens, P. (2006) 'Physical and sexual assault of women with disabilities.' *Violence Against Women 12*, 9, 823–836.

Mays, J. (2006) 'Feminist disability theory: Domestic violence against women with a disability.' *Disability & Society 21*, 2, 147–158.

McCarthy, M. (2000) *Sexuality and Women with Learning Difficulties*. London: Jessica Kingsley Publishers.

Mencap (2011) 'Attitudes to disability and hate crime: Topline results.' Available at www.mencap.org.uk, accessed on 5 July 2011.

Mirrlees-Black, C. (1999) *Domestic Violence: Findings from a New British Crime Survey Self-completion Questionnaire*. London: Home Office.

Morris, J. (ed.) (1996) *Encounters with strangers*. London: The Women's Press.

Mullender, A. and Hague, G. (2000) *Survivors' Views on Domestic Violence Services*. London: Home Office.

Mullender, A., Hague, G., Imam, U., Kelly, L., Malos, E. and Regan, L. (2002) *Children's Perspectives on Domestic Violence*. London: Sage Publications.

Mullender, A. and Morley, R. (1994) (eds) *Children Living with Domestic Violence: Putting Men's Abuse of Women on the Child Care Agenda.* London: Whiting and Birch.

Nixon, J. (2009) 'Domestic violence and women with disabilities: Locating the issue on the periphery of social movements.' *Disability and Society 24*, 1, 77–89.

Nosek M., Foley C., Hughes R. and Howland, C. (2001) 'Vulnerabilities for abuse among women with disabilities.' *Sexuality and Disability 19*, 3, 177–190.

Nosek, M. and Howland, C. (1998) 'Abuse and women with disabilities.' Harrisburg, PA: VAWnet, a project of the National Resource Center on Domestic Violence/Pennsylvania Coalition Against Domestic Violence. Available at www.vawnet.org/research/print-document.php?doc_id=369&find_type=web_desc_AR, accessed on 21 November 2010.

Nosek, M., Howland, C. and Young, M. (1997) 'Abuse of women with disabilities: Policy implications.' *Journal of Disability Policy Studies 8*, 157–176.

Nosek, M., Hughes, B. and Robinson-Whelen, S. (2007) 'Correlates of depression in rural women with physical disabilities.' *Journal of Obstetric, Gynecologic, & Neonatal Nursing 36*, 1, 105–114.

Nosek, M., Hughes, R., Taylor, H. and Taylor, P. (2006) 'Disability, psychosocial and demographic characteristics of abused women with physical disabilities.' *Violence Against Women 12*, 9, 838–850.

Novis, A. (2010) *The Bigger Picture.* London: United Kingdom Disabled People's Council. Available at www.ukdpc.net, accessed on 5 July 2011.

Oliver, M. (1996) *Understanding Disability: From Theory to Practice.* London: Macmillan.

Parekh, P. (ed.) (2007) 'Intersecting gender and disability perspectives.' *Wagadu: A Journal of Transnational Women's and Gender Studies,* Special Edition, Summer 2007. Available at wagadu.org/Volume%204/Articles%20Volume%204/Ediorial07.htm, accessed on 5 July 2011.

Powers, L., Curry, M., Oschwald, M., Maley, S., Eckels K. and Saxton, M. (2002) 'Barriers and strategies in addressing abuse within personal assistance relationships: A survey of disabled women's experiences.' *Journal of Rehabilitation 68*, 1, 4–13.

Radford, J., Harne, L. and Trotter, J. (2006) 'Disabled women and domestic violence as violent crime in practice.' *Journal of the British Association of Social Workers 18*, 4, 233–246.

Radford, L. and Hester, M. (2006) *Mothering through Domestic Violence.* London: Jessica Kingsley Publishers.

Saxton, M., Curry, M.A., Powers, L., Maley, S., Eckels, K. and Gross, J. (2001) 'Bring my scooter so I can leave you: A study of disabled women handling abuse by personal assistance providers.' *Violence Against Women 7*, 393–417.

Schechter, S. (1982) *Women and Male Violence: The Visions and Struggles of the Battered Women's Movement.* Boston: South End Press.

Scope/Disability Now/UK Disabled People's Council (2008) *Getting Away with Murder: Disabled People's Experience of Hate Crime in the UK.* London: Scope.

Shakespeare, T. (1998) *The Disability Reader: Social Science Perspective.* London: Cassell.

Shakespeare, T. and Watson, N. (1997) 'Defending the social model.' *Disability and Society 12*, 2, 293–300.

Smith, B. and Hutchison, B. (eds) (2006) *Gendering Disability.* Piscataway, NJ: Rutgers University Press.

Sobsey, D. (1994) *Violence in the Lives of People with Disabilities: The End of Silent Acceptance?* Baltimore: Brookes.

Social Care Institute for Excellence (2011) *Protecting Adults at Risk: London Multi-agency Policy and Procedures to Safeguard Adults from Abuse.* London: SCIE. Available at www.scie.org.uk/publications/reports/report39.asp, accessed on 5 July 2011.

Stark, E. (2007) *Coercive Control: How Men Entrap Women in Personal Life.* New York: Oxford University Press.

Stopes, M. (1920) *The Control of Parenthood.* Quoted on various websites, including www.nndb.com and Wikipedia, accessed on 5 July 2011.

Swain, J., Finkelstein, V., French, S. and Oliver, M. (eds) (2004) *Disabling Barriers – Enabling Environments.* London: Sage.

Swedlund, N. and Nosek, M. (2000) 'An exploratory study on the work of independent living centers to address the abuse of women with disabilities.' *Journal of Rehabilitation 66,* 4, 57–64.

Thiara, R.K. and Gill, A.K. (2010) 'Understanding Violence against South Asian Women: What It Means for Practice.' In R.K. Thiara and A.K. Gill (eds) *Violence against Women in South Asian Communities: Issues for Policy and Practice.* London: Jessica Kingsley Publishers.

Thiara, R.K., Hague, G. with Mullender, A. (2011 forthcoming) 'Losing out on both counts: Disabled women and domestic violence.' *Disability and Society 26,* 6.

Trotter, J., Radford, J. and Harne, L. (2007) 'Changing relationships: Services for disabled women experiencing domestic violence.' *Research, Policy and Training 25,* 2/3, 155–166.

UK Disability Forum (2008) *Information for Disabled Women about Getting Help to Tackle Violence and Abuse.* Available at www.edfwomen.org.uk/abuse.htm, accessed on 5 July 2011.

UK Disability Forum (2011) *Manifesto by Disabled Women in Europe.* Available at www.edfwomen.org.uk/manifesto.htm, accessed on 8 July 2011.

UPIAS (Union of the Physically Impaired Against Segregation) (1976) *Fundamental Principles of Disability.* London: UPIAS.

Vernon, A. (1997) 'Fighting Two Different Battles: Unity is Preferable to Enmity.' In L. Barton and M. Oliver (eds) *Disability Studies: Past, Present and Future.* Leeds: The Disability Press.

Vernon, A. (1998) 'Multiple Oppression and the Disabled People's Movement. In T. Shakespeare (ed.) *The Disability Reader: Social Science Perspectives.* London: Cassell.

Vernon, A. and Swain, J. (2002) 'Theorising Divisions and Hierarchies: Towards Commonality or Diversity?' In C. Barnes and M. Oliver (eds) *Disability Studies Today.* Bristol: Policy Press.

WHO (2005) *Multi-country Study of Health and Domestic Violence Against Women.* Geneva: WHO. Available at whqlibdoc.who.int/publications/2005/924159358X_eng.pdf, accessed on 5 July 2011.

WHO (2009) 'International Classification of Functioning, Disability and Health (ICF).' Available at www.WHO.int/classifications/icf, accessed on 5 July 2011.

Women With Disabilities Australia (WWDA) (1999) *More Than Just A Ramp – A Guide for Women's Refuges to Develop Disability Discrimination Act Action Plans.* Available for purchase at www.wwda.org.au/vrm2007.htm, accessed on 5 July 2011.

Women's Aid (2007) 'What is domestic violence?' Available at www.womensaid.org.uk/domestic-violence-articles.asp?section=00010001002200410001&itemid=1272&itemTitle=What+is+domestic+violence, accessed on 5 July 2011.

Young, M., Nosek, M., Howland, C., Campling, G. and Rintala, D. (1997) 'Prevalence of abuse of women with physical disabilities.' *Archives of Physical Medicine and Rehabilitation 78,* 534–538.

Yuval-Davis, N. (2006) 'Intersectionality and feminist politics.' *European Journal of Women's Studies 13,* 3, 193–209.

Reports

The key reports from the national study on which this book is based are:

Hague, G., Thiara, R., Magowan, P. and Mullender, A. (2008) *Making the Links: Disabled Women and Domestic Violence. Full Report.* Bristol: Women's Aid.

Hague, G., Thiara, R., Magowan, P. and Mullender, A. (2008) *Making the Links: Disabled Women and Domestic Violence. Good Practice Guide.* Bristol: Women's Aid.

These are summarised in the following papers:

Thiara, R. and Hague, G. with Mullender, A. (2011 forthcoming) 'Losing out on both counts: Disabled women and domestic violence.' *Disability and Society 26*, 6.

Hague, G., Thiara, R. and Mullender, A. (2011) 'Disabled women and domestic violence: Making the links, a national UK study.' *Psychiatry, Psychology and Law 18*, 1, 117.

Other reports on disabled women and domestic violence are available from:

www.womensaid.org.uk
www.bristol.ac.uk/sps/research/genderviolence
www.warwick.ac.uk/shss/swell

Subject Index

abuse 9, 13–14, 16–17, 33
  abuse by paid carers 45–6, 52,
    114, 137, 143, 154, 169,
    170–1
  effects 51–3
  emotional abuse 17, 26, 36, 42,
    51–2, 63
  financial abuse 17, 42, 45
  impairment-specific abuse
    40–1, 170
  mental abuse 63
  multiple and complex abuse
    35–8
  post-separation abuse 50–1
  response to abuse 47–9
  vulnerability 27–8, 29, 42–3,
    116–19, 132, 171–2
  see also domestic violence
accessibility 28, 32–3, 58, 64
  practice recommendations
    147–8
  social model of disability 88
accommodation 68
  adapted accommodation 28,
    44, 58, 64
Action Plan on violence against
  women and girls 103–4,
    161–2, 166
activists 9, 18, 19, 20, 23, 32, 110
  gender and inequality 29–31
  organisations 32, 90, 91
adult services 53, 69, 72–4, 138
Advisory Group 9, 174, 175
advocacy services 18, 120, 129,
    145
age 55
agencies 18, 137–8
  accessibility 32–3
  agency care 48–9
  need for change 138
  non-specialised agencies 78–9
  responses from formal agencies
    69–70
America see USA
Armstrong, Keith 90
Ashiana 91
Asian women 91
Askew, David 136
assault 17, 28–9, 38, 94, 104,
    110, 117, 124, 132, 136

Australia 14, 26, 27, 29, 31, 33,
    93, 177
awareness, raising 148–9
  public education 146–7

Bangladesh 17
Bashall, Ruth 23, 89–91, 136,
    137, 178
Beverley Lewis House 121–3, 129
Big Lottery Fund 9, 19
black women 22, 27, 30, 65,
    73–4, 91, 92–3, 113, 122,
    142, 175, 179
blind people 87
BMER (black, minority ethnic
  and refugee) 22, 27, 65, 67,
    137, 147, 150, 153, 165,
    175, 176
  domestic violence services 78
  disability organisations 74
  social services 73–4
Boadicea Disabled Women's Newsletter
    90, 96
Brazil 17
British Association of Disabled
  People's Organisations 136
British Council of Disabled People
    32
British Council of Organisations of
  Disabled People (BCODP)
    93, 97
British Crime Survey (BCS) 28–9
British Sign Language (BSL) 100,
    125, 147, 148, 177
Broken Rainbow 91
bullying 91, 111, 115, 125

CAADA 130, 132
Canada 14, 26, 93, 94
care packages 28, 58, 62, 108,
    125, 143, 160, 171
  portability 143, 146, 153, 154
  statutory sector 144–5
carers 22, 23, 27–9
  abuse by paid carers 45–6, 52,
    114, 137, 143, 154, 169,
    170–1
  abusive carers 27–9, 36, 131,
    143, 170
  abusive partner-carers 39–44,
    52, 63, 68

Centre for the Study of Safety and
  Well-being 19, 179
children 9, 13, 19, 23, 52, 53–5,
    61, 64
  child protection register 71
  disabled children 18, 87
  domestic violence 49–50
  foster care 74
  onset of abuse 38
children's services 13
Chile 17
China 17
Churchill, Winston 107
Citizens Advice Bureau 78
Comic Relief 97
Community Safety Units 119
counselling 13, 55, 58, 61, 79,
    130, 143
criminal justice system 13, 18, 28,
    109, 130
Criminal Records Bureau (CRB)
    120
Crown Prosecution Service 130,
    133, 136

Daisie Project 124, 135
DAWN (Disabled Women's
  Network) 26, 93, 94
Deaf 84, 87, 100, 101, 103, 126,
    128, 136
  adapted accommodation 148
  Deaf Women Against Violence
    124–5, 136
dementia 160
Department of Health 158, 160
depression 51, 52, 69
direct payments 46, 108, 170
disability 14
  disability and disabled people's
    organisations 60–2
  domestic violence services 18
  gender and inequality 29–31
  social versus medical model
    15–16, 83–5
  'solutions' 83, 105
Disability Action Waltham Forest
    91, 136
  Stay Safe project 95–6, 119,
    125–6
disability advisory groups 163–4

Disability Discrimination Acts
    (1995 and 2005) 59,
    100–1, 149
Disability Equality Schemes 100
Disability Independent Advisory
    Group (DIAG) 91, 164
disability organisations 60–2, 69,
    74–5, 129, 155–6
    Glasgow 124–5, 133, 135
    history 92–6
    practice recommendations
        140–1, 151–2
    strategic issues 168
    views and advice of disabled
        women 143–4
    working in partnership 133–4
Disability Rights Watch UK 105
Disabled Peoples' International
    (DPI) 93
disabled women 9, 10, 13–14, 17,
    18, 34–5, 82–3, 104, 106,
    137–8
    advice to others 79–80
    children 53–5
    effects of abuse 51–3
    help-seeking 62–6
    increased likelihood of assault
        28–9
    involvement in policy
        development 147
    involvement in service provision
        141–2
    living in an unequal world
        111–13
    outcomes of help-seeking 66–8
    response to abuse 47–9
    separation from abusers 49–51
    study 18–19, 22–3, 23–4
    study aims 20
    study conclusions 169–73
    study methods 20–2
    views and advice 142–3
    working in partnership 133–4
disbelief 29, 43, 154, 169
    DISBELIEF 123
discrimination 14, 30, 31, 84, 85,
    86, 87, 89, 90, 92, 93, 134,
    157, 164
    Deaf women 126
    Disability Discrimination Acts
        (1995 and 2005) 59,
        100–1, 149
    Equality Act 2010 101
    feminist definition 106, 107
    learning difficulties 117, 123
    UN Convention on the
        Rights of Persons with
        Disabilities 102
domestic violence 9, 13–14, 34–5,
    82–3
    Action Plan 103–4
    burden of caring' as motive 119
    children 49–50
    definition 16–17, 113–15
    disability services 18

inclusive approach 131
injuries 36
living in an unequal world
    111–13
reporting and getting help 128
study 18–19, 22–3, 23–4
study aims 20
study conclusions 169–73
study methods 20–2
wider definition 131
see also abuse
domestic violence services 18,
    57–60, 69, 75–8, 155–6
    practice recommendations
        140–1, 149–51
    strategic issues 168
    views and advice of disabled
        women 143–4

eating disorders 52
El Salvador 93
Ellis, Brenda 23, 85–9, 96, 137,
    178–9
England 57, 170, 174
Equality 2025 98–9
equality 9, 18, 23, 87, 172
    disability equality training
        59–60, 139, 140
    strategic issues 162–3, 167
Equality Act 2010 57, 101–2,
    149, 152, 162
Equality and Human Rights
    Commission 104, 125, 158
Equality Duty 101
Ethiopia 17
ethnicity 16, 21, 27, 31, 55
    staffing preferences 142
    see also BMER (black, minority
        ethnic and refugee)
European Disability Forum
    Women's Committee 97,
    98–9
exclusion 15, 16, 20, 84, 85, 87,
    88, 89, 133

family members 22, 23, 50, 66–7,
    114
    abusive family members 36,
        121
fear 52, 63, 64
feminism 86, 90, 92–6
    'Third Wave' 99
    understanding of violence
        106–7
feminists 9, 19, 30–1, 85, 89,
    107, 110
forced marriage 16, 132, 136
France 135
friends 66, 67

gays 16, 90, 91, 101, 106
gender 9, 55
Gender and Violence Research
    Centre 19

genital mutilation 161
Germany 93, 98
Gillespie-Sells, Kath 90
Glasgow 124–5, 135
Glasgow Disability Alliance 124
Glasgow Violence Against Women
    123–4
good practice see practice
    recommendations
government policies 13, 18, 19,
    101–2
    Action Plan on violence against
        women and girls 103–4,
        161–2
    spending cuts 83, 134, 139,
        140, 145, 156
GPs 69, 78, 79, 171
Greater London Action on
    Disability (GLAD) 32, 85–6,
    88, 89, 96–7
Greater London Domestic Violence
    Strategy 89, 96
Greece 135
Greenwich Association of Disabled
    People 136
Grothaus, Rebecca 94, 95
guilt 48, 68

Hague, Gill 179
harassment 110, 115, 125
Hardwick, Francesca 110, 136
hate crimes 91, 110, 114, 115,
    116, 125, 128, 134, 135,
    136
Hearn, Kirsten 90
helplines 33, 88, 89, 94, 143,
    148, 150
    National Domestic Violence
        Helpline 99, 100
Hershey, Laura 90, 105
holistic support 129
Home Office 95, 136, 158, 160
'honour' crimes 16, 116, 132
housing 13, 143
human rights 9, 84, 85, 104, 119,
    136, 163, 166

impairments 15, 22, 25
    categorisation 86
    impairment-specific abuse
        40–1, 170
independent living 92, 108–9,
    129
independent living centres 33
independent living reviews 46
Indonesia 17
information 128, 140–1, 148–9
Inglis, Frances 135
injunctions 72, 79
institutional abuse 90, 91, 96,
    114, 117, 120–1, 122,
    125, 178
institutional advocacy 71
institutional care 83, 129

institutionalisation 49, 62, 92, 94, 107–8, 112, 118, 121, 132, 142, 161
intermediaries 130, 136
International Women's Day 99
intersectionality 30–1, 55, 111, 137, 157
Islington 25
isolation 28, 29, 39–40, 62–3, 170
Italy 98

Japan 17

Kiran 91

labelling 84, 94, 109, 117
language problems 47, 137
LANGUID 90, 105
learning difficulties 22, 25, 83, 85, 108, 120, 135, 160
    abusive partners 88–9
    Beverley Lewis House 121–3
    discrimination 117, 123
    forced marriage 136
    refuges 100
    sexuality 112–13
Leeds City Council Domestic Violence Team 32, 123, 145, 164–5
    Minimum Standards Quality Mark 165
Leeds Inter-Agency Project (LIAP) 32, 123
legislation 100–1, 101–2
Lesbian Mothers Network 89
lesbians 16, 22, 27, 33, 65–6, 85, 90, 91, 101, 106, 137, 147, 150, 153, 172, 176
Lewis, Beverley 122
London Lesbian Line 89
London Public Attitude Survey 136
Lorde, Audre 90, 105
Luxemburg, Rosa 92

Making the Links 99, 103, 118
Manifesto by Disabled Women in Europe 98–9, 105
Martin, Brent 109
men 13, 16–17
mental health issues 22, 83, 85, 108, 120
Metropolitan Police 17, 91, 100–1
Middlesbrough 25
MIND 78
Ministry of Justice 91, 160
Montenegro 17
Mullender, Audrey 179
multi-agency risk assessment conferences (MARAC) 125, 135, 161
murder 109–10, 121, 161

Namibia 17
National Domestic Violence Helpline 99, 100
national surveys 56–7
    disability and disabled people's organisations 60–2
    domestic violence services 57–60
Nazism 107
neighbours 66, 68
New Zealand 17
Nicaragua 93
No Secrets 117, 120, 144, 152, 154, 160–1
non-verbal people 83, 120
North America 26
Novis, Anne, MBE 91

older women 22, 29, 108, 122, 147
oppression 29–31, 87, 90, 157
    internalised oppression 83
    social oppression 84–5, 107, 108, 146–7
outreach services 13, 18, 19, 21, 138
    accessibility 28, 140, 145

parents 66
partners 22, 27, 28
    abusive partner-carers 39–44, 52, 63
    abusive partners 121, 143
    ex-partners 22, 50–1
    partner-carers 55
    partner violence 35, 36
    separation from abusers 49–51
partnership 13, 133–4, 158–60
patriarchy 106–7
perpetrators 16, 21, 22, 23, 29, 169
personal assistants (PAs) 22, 39, 58, 62, 143, 154, 169
personal histories 85
    Bashall, Ruth 89–91
    Ellis, Brenda 85–9
Peru 17
physical impairments 15, 22, 25, 84, 85
Pilkington, Fiona 110, 136
police 17, 69, 101, 126, 133, 164, 171, 172
    Community Safety Units (CSUs) 119
    hate crime recording 135
    Leicestershire 110
    police responses 70–2, 130, 136
    Safer Neighbourhood teams 128
policy approaches 9–10
policy development 20, 22, 140, 141, 142
    involving disabled women in policy development 147

partnership working 158–60
    research 31–3
    UK 108–9
power issues 29, 170
Powerhouse 121–2
practice recommendations 24, 121, 134, 140–1, 176–7
    abusive carers 154
    accessibility of services 147–8
    Beverley Lewis House 121–3
    Daisie Project 124
    Deaf Women Against Violence 125
    disability organisations 151–2
    domestic violence organisations 149–51
    improvement of services 139–40
    inclusive approach to violence against women 131–2
    involving disabled women in policy development 147
    involving disabled women in service provision 141–2
    Leeds Inter-Agency Project 123
    need for change 138
    principles of good practice 126
    provision of services 145–6
    raising awareness 148–9
    social model of disability 126–30
    statutory sector 152–4
    Stay Safe 125–6
    strategic issues 166–8
    training and public education 146–7
    views and advice of disabled women 142–4
    working in partnership 133–4
practitioners 14, 18, 20, 22, 24
Pridmore, Anne 97
privacy 45–6
professionals 9, 23, 24, 56, 80–1, 118, 171
    adult services and social care 72–4
    disability organisations 74–5
    domestic violence services 75–8
    national surveys 56–62
    non-specialised agencies 78–9
    outcomes of help-seeking 66–8
    police responses 70–2
    responses from formal agencies 69–70
    training 139
    women's help-seeking 62–6
public spending cuts 83, 134, 139, 140, 145, 156
publicity 140–1

quality marks 165, 167–8
Quarmby, Katharine 110

racism 30, 65, 106, 157
rape 17, 28, 38, 89, 90, 110, 116,
    120, 122, 124, 136, 161
recovery 130
Refuge 99
refuges 13, 17, 18, 19, 21, 69,
    126
    accessibility 58, 76, 88, 89, 91,
        94, 99, 100, 140, 145
    Beverley Lewis House 121–3
    provision of services 128–9
    UK Refuges Online 57, 81,
        174–5
research 25–7
    gender and inequality 29–31
    isolation 28, 29
    power issues 29
    service provision and policy
        31–3
    vulnerability 27–8, 29
residential homes 22, 49, 120–1
Rights Now 86
risk assessment 132
risk minimisation 108, 131

safeguarding 32, 104, 116, 117,
    170
    domestic violence 119–21
    Safeguarding Adults 114,
        120–1, 135, 160–1
Safer Neighbourhood teams 128
safety, personal 79, 123, 124,
    142–3, 148
Samoa 17
Sanctuary 129
Scandinavia 98
Scope 32
Scotland 25, 124
self-blame 48, 94
sensory impairments 22, 25,
    84, 85
Serbia 17
services 9, 13, 19, 20, 22–3, 24,
    137–8
    accessibility of services 147–8
    care packages 144–5
    improvement of services
        139–40
    need for integration 18, 138
    practice recommendations
        145–6
    research 31–3
sexism 30, 157
sexual abuse 52, 115
sexual violence 9, 17, 38, 104,
    110, 124, 132, 136
sexuality 21, 26, 43, 55, 170
    learning difficulties 112–13
shame 43, 48, 94, 109
Shellard, Louise 91
siblings 66
sign language 28, 100, 125, 147,
    148, 177

Sisters Against Disablement (SAD)
    92, 93
social model of disability 15–16,
    83–5, 169–70
    accessibility 88
    criminal justice system 130
    holistic support 129
    inclusive approach 126–8,
        130–2
    information 128
    learning and training 130
    refuges 128–9
    reporting and getting help 128
    short-term and long-term
        recovery 130
    working in partnership 133–4
social services 18, 32–3, 61, 69,
    72–4, 138, 172
    children 53, 54, 61
societal attitudes 15, 28, 29
socio-economic status 21
solicitors 69, 72, 78, 171
South Asian women 22, 31, 136,
    175, 176
Southall Black Sisters 92
Spain 98, 177
special needs 29, 83, 85, 100, 116
special schools 87, 112, 127, 135
speech impairment 101
statistics 57, 81, 160
statutory sector 18, 20, 32, 65,
    68, 72, 81, 120, 156, 158,
    170, 172
    care packages 144–5
    practice recommendations
        152–4
    response 131, 138, 155
    safeguarding policies 120, 121
Stopes, Marie 107
strategic issues 156
    Action Plan on violence against
        women and girls 161–2
    basic considerations 157
    disability advisory groups
        163–4
    disability organisations 168
    domestic violence organisations
        168
    domestic violence quality marks
        and minimum standards
        167–8
    domestic violence strategies and
        equality 167
    equality 162–3, 167
    Leeds City Council Domestic
        Violence Team 164–5
    local strategic work 162, 163
    No Secrets 160–1
    partnership working 13,
        158–60
    Safeguarding Adults 114,
        120–1, 135, 160–1
    strategic and commissioning
        frameworks 166–7
    study investigations 157

study 18–19, 20–2, 22–3, 23–4,
    157–8, 174–7
Supporting People programme
    166, 168
survivors 9, 10, 19
Sweden 105, 177

Tanzania, United Republic of 17
Thailand 17
Thiara, Ravi 179
tokenism 19, 133, 172
training 130, 139, 140, 141
    practice recommendations
        146–7
transport 28, 58, 85, 88, 90, 93
    public transport 83, 87, 90,
        116
trust 52, 63, 73–4, 75, 115
    expectation of trust 114
Truth, Sojourner 92

UK 13, 14, 15, 17, 18, 19, 22,
    33, 98–9, 103, 112
    history of disability
        organisations 92–6
    policy developments 108–9
    research 25–7, 28–9, 31
UK Disability Forum Women's
    Committee 32, 86, 97–8
UK Disabled People's Council
    (UKDPC) 32, 57, 134, 174
UK Refuges Online (UKROL) 57,
    81, 174–5
Union of the Physically Impaired
    Against Segregation (UPIAS)
    92
United Kingdom Disabled People's
    Council 105, 110
United Nations Convention on
    the Rights of Persons with
    Disabilities 93, 102–3, 105
University of Bristol 19, 21
University of Warwick 19, 21
unworthiness 43, 51
USA 14, 26, 29, 31, 33, 93

Vietnam 17
violence 104, 106
    appropriate terminology
        110–11
    attitudes to disabled people
        107–9, 110–11
    feminist perspective 106–7
    see also domestic violence; sexual
        violence
Violence Against Women Research
    Group 19
Violence Against Women Service
    Development Fund 124
visual impairment 84, 148
Voice UK 136
vulnerability 27–8, 29, 42–3,
    116–19, 132, 171–2

Wagadu 30
Waltham Forest 25
websites 32–3, 91, 97–8, 99, 123
wheelchair users 27, 37, 40–1,
    100
  acquired impairment 86, 90
Wise Women 124, 125, 135
women 9, 13, 16–17, 19
Women with Disabilities Australia
    (WWDA) 93
Women's Aid 9, 10, 16, 17, 58,
    99–100, 126, 140, 151,
    155, 169
  national surveys 56–7
  posters 128
  statistics 57, 81, 160
  study 18–19, 22–3, 23–4
  study aims 20
  study interviews 157–8, 175–6
  study methods 20–2, 174–7

Author Index

ABS 29
ACPO 113
Aris, R. 19
Asch, A. 29

Barron, J. 99
Bashall, R. 115
BCODP 97
Begum, N. 27, 92, 95
Brisenden, S. 15
Brookes, S. 110, 111
Browne, S.E. 94
Brownridge, D. 26

CAADA 132
Campling, J. 93
Chang, J. 31
Charlton, J. 16
Chenoweth, L. 18, 26, 27, 28, 29, 31
Clements, N. 26
Cockram, J. 27, 31
Connors, D. 94
Cook, S. 26
Corker, M. 15
Cosgrove, K. 25
Cramer, E. 25
Crenshaw, K. 30
Cross, M. 28
Crow, L. 83

Daily Mail 135
Daisie Project 124, 135
Daley, M. 99
Deaf Women Against Violence 136
Department of Health 117, 144, 152, 160, 161
Depoy, E. 25
Disability Now 109
DisAbled Women's Network (DAWN) 28, 94
Dobash, R. 20
Dorian, P.N. 26
Dullea, K. 23

Ellis, B. 19, 32
Ellis, R. 136
Equality and Human Rights Commission (EHRC) 101, 104, 115, 117, 118

Fine, M. 29
Flatley, J. 136
Foreign and Commonwealth Office 136

French, S. 95

Gadd, D. 16
Gangoli, G. 16
Garland-Thompson, R. 26
Gill, A.K. 30, 31, 35, 157
Gilson, S. 25
Goode, A. 136
Greater London Action on Disability (GLAD) 96
Guardian 110

Hague, G. 13, 17, 19, 20, 22, 23, 30, 99
Hannaford, S. 93
Harne, L. 13, 19
Hassouneh-Phillips, D. 29
Healey, D. 27, 33
Hester, M. 16, 119
Hill, F. 25
HM Government 103, 161
Home Office 117, 144, 152, 160, 161
Horvath, M. 35
Howe, K. 33
Howland, C. 26
Hughes, B. 26
Humphreys, C. 28
Hurst, R. 84
Hutchison, B. 30

James-Hanman, D. 13, 18–19, 25, 28, 31
Jansson, K. 29
Jennings C. 111

Kelly, L. 35

Leeds Inter-Agency Project (LIAP) 123
Lisney, E. 99
London Metropolitan Police 114

Macleod, J. 25
Magowan, P. 20, 27, 28, 29, 32, 33
Malos, E. 13, 17, 20
Martin, S. 26, 29
Mays, J. 30
McCarthy, M. 25
McCarry, M. 16
Mencap 108, 135
Mirrlees-Black, C. 29
Morris, J. 30, 92, 95

Mullender, A. 19, 23, 30, 53
Morley, R. 53

Nixon, J. 18, 29, 30, 31, 34, 35
Nosek, M. 26, 27, 28, 33, 35
Novis, A. 110
NPIA 113

Oliver, M. 15

Parekh, P. 30
Powers, L. 29

Radford, J. 13, 19, 25, 31, 32, 34, 35, 39, 119
Razak, A. 16
Robinson-Whelan, S. 26

Saxton, M. 27–8, 29, 45
Schechter, S. 20
Scope 109
Shakespeare, T. 15, 16, 30
Smith, B. 30
Sobsey, D. 27, 28
Social Care Institute for Excellence 120
Stark, E. 16
Stern, N. 94
Stopes, M. 107
Swain, J. 16, 30
Swedlund, N. 33

Thiara, R.K. 28, 30, 31, 35, 157
Thomas, C. 15
Trotter, J. 13, 18, 19, 25, 31, 32

UK Disability Forum 32, 97, 105
UK Disabled People's Council 109
UPIAS (Union of the Physically Impaired Against Segregation) 15

Vernon, A. 27, 30, 31

Watson, N. 15, 16
WHO (World Health Organisation) 15, 17, 20
Wise Women 136
Women With Disabilities Australia (WWDA) 105
Women's Aid 16, 17, 113

Young, M. 26, 35
Yuval-Davis, N. 30